Option Income Strategy Trade Filters

An In-Depth Article Demonstrating the Use of Trade Filters to Enhance Returns and Reduce Risk

BRIAN JOHNSON

ISBN-10: 0-9961823-1-4
ISBN-13: 978-0-9961823-1-7

DISCLAIMER

Information in this article is provided solely for informational and general educational purposes and should not be construed as an offer to sell or the solicitation of an offer to buy securities or to provide investment advice. Option trading has large potential rewards, but also large potential risk. You must be aware of the risks and be willing to accept them in order to invest in the options markets. Do not trade with money you cannot afford to lose. Historical results are not necessarily indicative of future performance.

COVER IMAGE

The fractal image on the cover is a graphical metaphor for the hidden relationships that influence the behavior of the financial markets – relationships that can be identified, quantified, and exploited by dedicated and resourceful traders.

CONTENTS

INTRODUCTION

Brian Johnson, a professional investment manager with many years of trading and teaching experience, is the author of two pioneering books on options: 1) *Option Strategy Risk / Return Ratios: A Revolutionary New Approach to Optimizing, Adjusting, and Trading Any Option Income Strategy*, and 2) *Exploiting Earnings Volatility: An Innovative New Approach to Evaluating, Optimizing, and Trading Option Strategies to Profit from Earnings Announcements.*

His new in-depth (100+ page) article, *Option Income Strategy Trade Filters,* represents the culmination of years of research into developing a systematic framework for optimizing the timing of Option Income Strategy (OIS) trades. His research was based on the analysis of 15,434 OIS trades, each with a comprehensive set of objective, tradable entry and exit rules. The results for each of the 15,000 plus trades were scaled to a constant dollar amount at risk, to ensure all trades were equally-weighted when calculating the performance metrics.

The back-test results were all based on actual option prices and are summarized in this article for a selection of back-testing filters, making this one of the most comprehensive studies of option income strategy results ever published. The results of over 100 different back-tests are provided.

The OIS strategy back-test results for ten different types of filters are evaluated in this article, including unique filter combinations that delivered exceptional results. A custom market-edge hypothesis was created in advance for each filter type, which was then used to evaluate the filter-specific results. This critical step helped identify robust, exploitable relationships, rather than spurious correlations.

Several of the resulting filters generated over 95% winning trades, with average returns of over six percent per trade (including losing trades). The ratios of cumulative gains to cumulative losses were over 20 to 1 for a few of the best performing filters.

Option Income Strategy Trade Filters is written in a clear, understandable fashion and provides detailed examples of how to create and test market-edge hypotheses using the recent advances in back-testing software. Very few formulas were included. As a result, the material in the article should be accessible to all option traders.

Useful for traders with a wide range of option trading experience, this practical guide begins with a detailed review of option income strategies, including basic examples that provide the requisite foundation for subsequent chapters. Portions of this crucial background material also appeared in Brian Johnson's first book: *Option Strategy Risk / Return Ratios.*

Chapter 2 includes a comprehensive description of the option income strategy, position model, and trade plan used to generate the back-test data. Every entry and exit rule is explained in detail, including actual graphical examples. The performance metrics for the 15,434 unfiltered OIS trades are summarized at the end of this chapter, which provide a performance benchmark for evaluating the effectiveness of the trade filters introduced in the next three chapters.

The trade filters are grouped by classification, with a chapter devoted to each class or type. The market-edge hypotheses and corresponding results for trend filters are analyzed in Chapter 3. Unlike trend filters, discriminating filters exclude an increasing percentage of trades as the filter condition or threshold becomes more extreme or restrictive. The discriminating filter market-edge hypotheses and results are analyzed in Chapter 4. Chapter 5 is devoted entirely to a very unique and powerful example of a discriminating filter: the OIS Universal Filter (OISUF).

The final chapter examines practical considerations and prospective applications of trade filters and other resources in managing option income strategies in actual market conditions.

1 - REVIEW

Before we can explore trade filters, we must first review option income strategies, option valuation, and the source of excess returns. Portions of the following crucial background material also appeared in my first book: *Option Strategy Risk / Return Ratios.*

Option Income Strategies

Market-neutral option income strategies are incredibly popular for one simple reason: they make money. What are market-neutral strategies? Market-neutral means that these strategies are neither bullish nor bearish. Market-neutral or non-directional strategies perform equally well, regardless whether the underlying security experiences a comparable increase or decrease in price.

This is very different from directional strategies that only earn positive returns when the market moves in the forecasted direction. Most traders focus almost exclusively on directional strategies. They may vary the holding periods, investment candidates, or technical triggers, but they allocate the majority of their capital to strategies that only earn a profit if the market moves in the desired direction.

As a result, market-neutral strategies offer significant strategy diversification benefits. When the market is trending, directional strategies tend to perform well, but option-income strategies do not. Conversely, during periods of price consolidation, directional strategies often underperform, but option-income strategies do very well. Consequently, allocating capital to both market-neutral and directional strategies can increase your returns and reduce your risk.

This probably seems strange to directional traders. If the market does not move, option income strategies make money. That's right, nothing happens, but you still make money. Unfortunately, option income strategies are complex. There are many exotic sounding option income strategies to choose from: iron butterflies, iron condors, double diagonals, calendar spreads, road trip, weirdor, and many others. Each of these strategies can be constructed from options with a wide range of strike prices and expiration dates, resulting in an overwhelming number of choices for the option trader.

I primarily use equity index options for my option income strategies. Equity index options are extremely liquid and the prices of equity indices are typically much higher than the prices of their corresponding exchange traded funds (ETFs). For example, the price of the S&P 500 index (SPX) is approximately ten times the price of its corresponding ETF (SPY).

As a result, one option contract on SPX is equivalent to approximately ten option contracts on SPY, but the commissions per contract are comparable. Therefore, the commissions from trading options on SPY are nearly ten times the cost of commissions from trading options on SPX. Using large, liquid equity indices for option income strategies reduces transaction costs, which is critical to the success of these multi-leg positions.

Equity index options also offer tax advantages and simplified IRS reporting requirements. In addition, equity indices are not as exposed to earnings spikes or specific company event risk, both of which could lead to large, discrete price changes that would be treacherous for most option income strategies. For the above reasons, I focus almost exclusively on the S&P 500 Index (SPX), the Russell 2000 Index (RUT) and the NASDAQ 100 Index (NDX) in this article.

In my first book, I provided the tools required to objectively evaluate any option income strategy, on any underlying security, in any market environment. However, I neglected to answer two important and related questions: when is the best time to employ option income strategies and when should they be avoided? I will demonstrate how to use objective filters to answer these questions in subsequent chapters, but first we need to examine how and why option income strategies make money. The secret is in the asymmetrical payoff function.

Asymmetrical Payoff Functions

The key to understanding option valuation is asymmetrical payoff functions, which are shared by both call and put options. This sounds complicated, but is actually relatively straightforward. A call option gives the owner or buyer the right, but not the obligation, to purchase the underlying asset at the strike price on or before the expiration date. For now, let's keep things simple and ignore the fact that many options can be exercised prior to expiration. This will allow us to focus our attention on what happens at option expiration.

The following example (depicted in Figure 1.1 below) should help illustrate the concept of asymmetry. If we purchased a one-year call option on IBM with a strike price of $100, we would only choose to exercise the call option if the price of IBM were above the $100 strike price (in the money) on the expiration date.

If the price of IBM were $110 on the expiration date, the payoff would be $10. The payoff to the option buyer is also called the intrinsic value and represents the value of exercising the in-the-money options at expiration. In this case, we could purchase IBM for the $100 strike price and immediately sell it at the market price of $110 for a payoff of $10. If the market price of IBM were $120 on the expiration date, the payoff would be $20. For every dollar the price of IBM rose above the strike price of $100, the payoff of the call option would increase by $1. As a result, the slope of the payoff function above the strike price is plus 1.0 (one dollar increase in payoff for every one dollar increase in the price of IBM).

If the price of IBM were below the $100 strike price (out of the money) on the expiration date, we would choose not to exercise the option and it would expire worthless. In that scenario, the payoff would be zero – although we would incur a loss on the trade.

It is important not to confuse payoffs and profits. Payoff functions (not profit and loss functions) should be used to determine the value of options. It would not matter how much the price of IBM dropped below $100; the call option would expire worthless and the payoff would still be zero. All options that are out of the money on the expiration date expire worthless and therefore have an intrinsic value and payoff of zero. As a result, the slope of the payoff function below the strike price is zero (zero change in the payoff function for a one dollar increase in the price of the underlying security).

Note the discrete change in the slope of the payoff function that occurs at the strike price. The slope of the light-colored payoff function is zero when the price of the underlying stock (IBM) is below the strike price ($100) and the slope of the payoff function line is plus 1.0 when the price of the stock is above the strike price. This payoff function is asymmetric and this asymmetry creates value for the call option. To understand how income strategies make money, we need to examine how this asymmetry creates value and how and why that value changes over time.

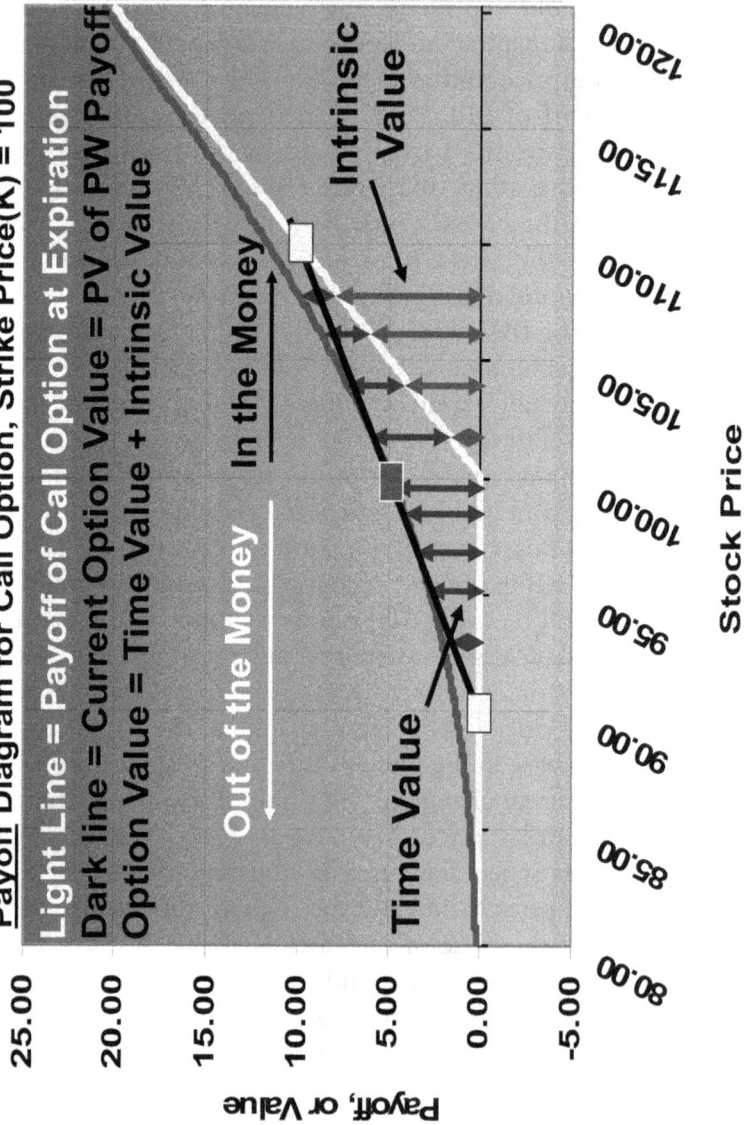

Figure 1.1: Call Option Payoff Diagram

Asymmetry & Option Values

The value of an option represents the present value of its probability-weighted future payoffs. What does that mean? Let's use the IBM call option payoff function from Figure 1.1 again to work through a simple example. First, let's assume that the stock price of IBM today is $100 and that one year from today, there were only two possible states of the world: the price of IBM would either increase by 10% (+ $10) or the price of IBM would decrease by 10% (- $10). In other words, one year from today there would be a 50% probability of IBM closing at $90 and a 50% probability of IBM closing at $110.

The payoffs in those two hypothetical scenarios would be $0 and $10, respectively (see yellow boxes in Figure 1.1 above). Given that the two possible payoffs of $0 and $10 both had a 50% probability of occurring, the average payoff one year from today would be $5 [(50% x $0) + (50% x $10)]. To determine the value of the call option today, we would technically need to discount the probability-weighted payoff of $5 back to the present using a proxy for the risk-free interest rate.

However, as I write this, short-term interest rates are near zero and have been approximately zero for several years. Even more important, discounting the expected future payoff would complicate our example unnecessarily and shift our focus away from our primary objective: understanding the effects of asymmetric payoff functions on option values.

To summarize the valuation example, IBM is currently trading at $100. If there were a 50% probability of IBM increasing or decreasing by 10% in one year, the value of a one-year call option with a strike price of $100 would be $5 (ignoring discounting).

Now we are finally ready to understand what happens to option values as time passes, which is the basis for all market-neutral option income strategies. Continuing with our IBM example, let's now assume that six months had passed and the price of IBM had remained unchanged at $100. The original one-year call option would now only have six months remaining until expiration. Assuming the market volatility environment had not changed, would the expected price change of IBM over the next six months be greater or less than our original 12-month assumed price change of plus or minus 10%?

It would be logical to assume that if IBM were expected to

increase or decrease by 10% over 12 months, IBM would be expected to increase or decrease by a lesser amount over six months, perhaps by only 5%. The assumption is logical, but the math would be a little different. I will address the math shortly, but for now, let's assume that IBM was expected to increase or decrease by 5% over the remaining six months.

The call option payoffs in those two new six-month scenarios would be $0 and $5, respectively. Using the same probability assumptions, the average payoff six months from today would be $2.50 [(50% x $0) + (50% x $5)]. If we ignore discounting again in our simplistic example, the value of the IBM call option would have declined from $5 to $2.50.

Since the market price of IBM was exactly equal to the strike price ($100), the intrinsic value would have been zero in both examples. However, the time premium or time value of the original one-year option would have declined by $2.50 over the six-month holding period.

The expected dispersion of prices decreases as time passes, which reduces the value of the asymmetrical payoff function, which means that option values decline over time. This is called time decay and it is measured by Theta.

This is how option income strategies make money. They make time decay work to their advantage by selling options (time value or time premium) and managing those positions as the time premium shrinks.

As is evident in this simple example, option prices are a direct function of the expected level of price volatility. As the expected level of volatility increases, the values of both call and put options also increase. The reason is asymmetry. Increasing volatility magnifies the value of asymmetry. Decreasing volatility diminishes the value of asymmetry.

Time Decay

As I mentioned above, the time decay function is actually not linear, unlike our simplistic assumption above. The expected dispersion of the price of the underlying security in most option models is not limited to two possible outcomes and it is not assumed to be a linear function of time. Instead, price dispersion and time premium are assumed to be increasing functions of the *square root of time*, not of time itself. In other words, the expected dispersion of prices over four months is NOT four times the expected dispersion of prices over one month. In practice, the expected dispersion of prices over four months is assumed to be *twice* (square root of 4) the expected dispersion of prices over one month.

Figure 1.2 below is a graph of the value of an at-the-money (ATM) call option (dotted line) and an ATM put option (dashed line) as a function of time. Time-to-expiration is depicted on the x-axis (horizontal) and the theoretical values of the call and put option relate to the left-hand y-axis (vertical).

Finally, the solid line represents the square root of the number of days until expiration and these values correspond to the right-hand y-axis (vertical). As you can see from the graph, the values of call and put options are clearly both a function of the square root of time remaining until expiration.

Since the call and put options in Figure 1.2 are at-the-money options, the intrinsic value is zero by definition. That means that the data depicted in the chart represents time value exclusively. Time value decays as a function of the square root of time, so selling time premium is the foundation of option income strategies. But which options should you sell?

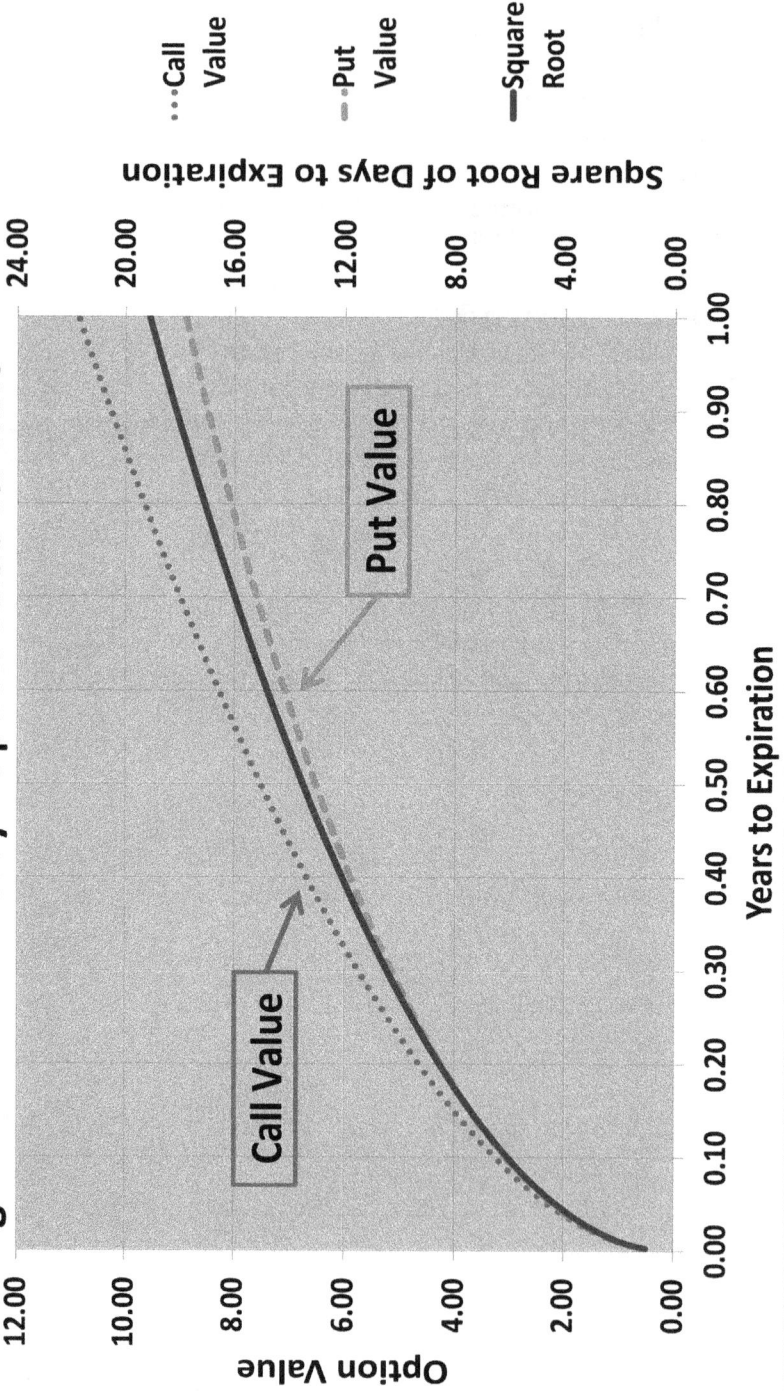

Figure 1.2: Time Decay - Option Value vs. Time

ATM options have the greatest time premium, so it would be logical to sell ATM or near-the-money options and buy out-of-the-money (OTM) options. If selling options allows you to profit from the decay of time value, why buy options at all? Because selling uncovered or naked options would expose you to unacceptable levels of risk and would also require excessive amounts of capital, which would reduce your prospective strategy returns.

As a result, option income strategies typically buy options further out of the money to "cover" their short option positions, which limits their prospective losses and reduces the margin requirement. This reduces the amount of capital required to implement the strategy, reduces risk, and also increases returns. Condors and Butterflies both buy OTM options to cover their short option positions.

However, there is another important insight that can be gleaned from the graph in Figure 1.2: time premium decays more rapidly as options approach expiration. As a result, it would be possible to benefit from time decay by selling an option with less time remaining and buying an option of the same type with more time remaining. This is called a calendar or time spread and it is another tool used in option income strategies.

Proven Option Income Advantage

The fact that options decay over time does not guarantee success or profitability for option income strategies. Selling options, even covered options, involves taking risk. In order to earn excess returns from selling options over time, options must be systematically and consistently overpriced. Many traders overlook this very important point. Are there any reasons that options would be systematically overpriced and are there any empirical data to support that theory? Absolutely.

The most compelling explanation as to why equity index options are chronically overvalued is that traders and investment managers use options to hedge their exposure to the market. There are only two types of traders: hedgers and speculators. Hedging transactions reduce risk and speculative transactions increase risk. In exchange for reducing risk, hedgers are willing to pay a premium when purchasing options. In exchange for taking on a portion of the hedger's risk, speculators (option sellers) demand a premium, just as insurance companies price their policies to earn a profit.

However, not every underlying security is used for hedging purposes, which means options are not systematically overvalued on all underlying securities. Option income strategies should only be employed using options that are chronically overvalued; this guarantees a proven statistical advantage.

How can you determine which underlying securities have options that have historically been overvalued? The easiest way is to compare implied volatility to statistical (also called historical) volatility. When implied volatility is consistently higher than statistical volatility, options for the underlying security are systematically overvalued, which creates a trading advantage for option sellers.

Statistical volatility is expressed as the annualized standard deviation of the percentage price change and is calculated from the actual price changes of the underlying security. Implied volatility is also expressed as the annualized standard deviation of the percentage price change, but it is not calculated from the actual price changes of the underlying security. Instead, it represents the expected level of volatility (price dispersion) that is priced into a specific option. In other words, implied volatility is the level of volatility that is implied by the price of the option; implied volatility is synonymous with option price.

As we saw in the IBM example, higher levels of expected volatility result in higher option prices. Conversely, lower levels of expected volatility mean lower option prices. This applies to both calls and puts. Higher implied volatility always equates to higher option prices and vice versa. The reason: higher expected volatility increases the expected value of asymmetry.

When the expected level of volatility priced into an option (implied volatility) is consistently higher than the actual volatility realized over the life of that option, the option would be systematically overvalued. The dashed line in Figure 1.3 below represents the statistical volatility (SV) for the S&P 500 index from 2010 through late 2013. The solid line represents the 30-day implied volatility (IV) for options on the S&P 500 index. As you can see from the chart, IV and SV tended to move together, but IV was consistently higher than SV.

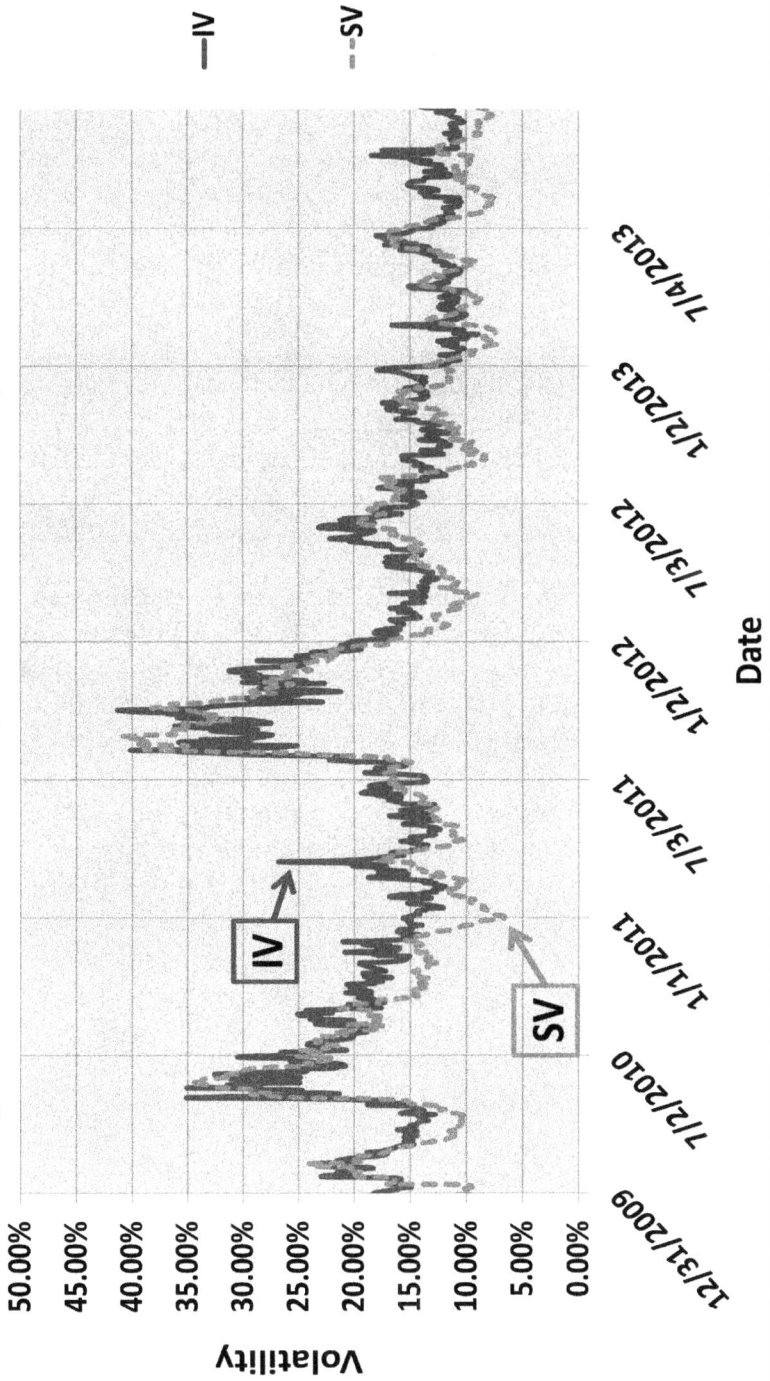

Figure 1.3: Implied (IV) & Statistical (SV) Volatility

The chart in Figure 1.3 above clearly demonstrates the historical relationship between IV and SV for S&P 500 index options, but it does not tell us the actual numerical difference between IV and SV. The average IV and SV values for the data in the above chart are provided in Figure 1.4 below.

The IV and SV averages were calculated for seven periods ranging from three weeks to six years. In every case, average implied volatility exceeded average statistical volatility for S&P 500 index options. The average difference between implied volatility and historical volatility across all periods was 2.05%.

Figure 1.4: S&P 500 Implied Volatility (IV) vs. Statistical Volatility (SV)							
Historical Period	3 Weeks	6 Weeks	10 Weeks	1.5 Years	3 Years	4.5 Years	6 Years
Implied Volatility (IV)	11.80%	11.50%	12.10%	13.20%	16.30%	17.70%	21.30%
Statistical Volatility (SV)	8.50%	8.80%	9.80%	11.70%	14.70%	15.80%	20.20%
Difference (IV - SV)	3.30%	2.70%	2.30%	1.50%	1.60%	1.90%	1.10%

At first glance, a difference of 2.05% might not seem significant. However, a 2.05% difference between IV and SV does not mean that options were only overvalued by 2.05%. Overestimating volatility by 2.05% would result in 30-day ATM call and put options that were overpriced by approximately 15%.

The objective of option income strategies is to harvest some of that 15% overvaluation. And the opportunity to capture that excess return is available every month. The introduction of weekly options opened up even more income strategy opportunities. I hope you are beginning to see the amazing return potential of employing option income strategies on underlying securities with systematically overvalued options.

The IV and SV data from Figures 1.3 and 1.4 were provided by OptionVue. For more information about OptionVue, please see the Resources Chapter at the end of this book.

Additional Evidence of a Trading Edge

The six-year relationship between IV and SV on S&P 500 index options is noteworthy, but in my proprietary research on option income strategies, I developed a tool that provided comprehensive evidence of a statistical advantage to selling options on equity indices.

I began with the following question: what is the probability advantage of selling out-of-the-money (OTM) equity index options as a function of 1) the length of the holding period and 2) the degree each option is out of the money.

I could have calculated the realized probabilities of each option expiring worthless (out of the money) and compared that to the tail probabilities from a normal distribution function. The simplicity of this approach was appealing, but the implications were simply not practical. This approach implicitly assumed that I would leave short option positions open, even after they moved in the money, hoping that prices would reverse and they would eventually expire worthless. The risk of this trading strategy would be unacceptable.

As a result, I instead calculated the realized probabilities of the price of the underlying security "touching" the strike price of the OTM option sold any time during the holding period. I then compared the realized touch probabilities to the theoretical probabilities of touching the short strike to determine the historical probability advantage or disadvantage. The mechanical details of calculating the theoretical touch probabilities are beyond the scope of this book, but the calculations used 5000-path Monte Carlo simulations from an arbitrage-free binomial lattice.

The following probabilities were calculated on the S&P 500 (SPX), Russell 2000 (RUT), and NASDAQ 100 (NDX) indices from 2000 through late 2013, using rolling holding periods ranging from one day to 60 days. Rolling holding periods means that a new holding period began every day, which means the holding periods overlapped. This provided more observations (over 9000), although the overlapping observations were not independent.

I chose the year 2000 as the starting point to ensure that two bull and two bear cycles were represented in the data. There was still an upward price bias in the equity indices from 2000 through 2013, but that is consistent with the performance of equity indices over most long-term periods.

For each holding period, I calculated the probability advantage of selling OTM options from 0.25 standard deviations (SD) out of the money to 2.0 SD out of the money, in 0.25 SD increments. The probability advantage equals the theoretical (Monte Carlo) probability of touching the strike price of the option sold, minus the realized probability of touching the same strike price.

Remember, when selling options, we would prefer that the theoretical probability of touching the short strike price be greater than the realized probability of touching the short strike. When this probability difference (theoretical – actual) was positive, that indicated a historical trading advantage. When this probability difference was negative, this signified a trading disadvantage.

The table of probability advantages for selling *OTM put options* is shown in Figure 1.5 and the table of probability advantages for selling *OTM call options* is presented in Figure 1.6 below. The historical probability advantage of selling OTM put options was remarkable. I had to run the analysis several times to finally convince myself the results were accurate. Part of the advantage obviously stems from the fact that equity prices have an upward bias, but selling OTM put options on equity indices has a definite trading edge.

Figure 1.5: OTM Short Put Probability Advantage										
#σ/#Days	1	2	3	4	5	6	10	15	20	40	60
0.250	11.80%	8.94%	7.93%	7.22%	7.04%	6.83%	6.75%	6.68%	6.91%	5.84%	5.80%
0.500	9.37%	8.05%	7.12%	6.86%	6.52%	6.64%	6.79%	7.62%	7.83%	7.39%	7.43%
0.750	9.32%	7.71%	7.47%	7.58%	7.79%	7.93%	9.00%	10.36%	10.82%	10.18%	10.10%
1.000	8.38%	7.94%	8.06%	8.71%	8.96%	9.67%	12.41%	13.70%	12.73%	12.01%	11.61%
1.250	8.20%	8.04%	8.55%	9.15%	9.51%	10.38%	12.89%	13.56%	12.82%	12.48%	11.68%
1.500	6.99%	7.35%	7.91%	8.38%	9.11%	9.48%	10.60%	11.05%	10.79%	10.72%	10.11%
1.750	5.36%	5.75%	6.37%	6.85%	7.16%	7.28%	7.80%	8.30%	8.00%	7.60%	7.20%
2.000	3.87%	4.16%	4.43%	4.64%	4.77%	4.77%	5.31%	5.60%	5.39%	4.95%	4.57%

Given the upward price bias in equity indices, it is no surprise that the probability edge from selling OTM call options is not as impressive (Figure 1.6 below). In fact, for most holding periods, there was a historical disadvantage to selling OTM call options within 0.50 SD from the current price. That disadvantage extended to 0.75 SD for longer holding periods (10 to 60 days).

Figure 1.6 OTM Short Call Probability Advantage										
#σ/#Days	1	2	3	4	5	6	10	15	20	40	60
0.250	8.19%	4.63%	2.32%	1.37%	0.97%	0.06%	-1.66%	-2.19%	-2.75%	-4.36%	-4.86%
0.500	6.21%	3.55%	1.34%	-0.16%	-0.58%	-1.30%	-3.10%	-4.77%	-5.61%	-6.47%	-6.70%
0.750	7.44%	4.17%	2.73%	1.65%	1.44%	0.83%	-0.90%	-2.19%	-3.07%	-3.13%	-3.47%
1.000	7.66%	5.58%	4.61%	4.59%	3.53%	3.21%	2.80%	2.49%	1.91%	1.78%	1.18%
1.250	6.62%	6.04%	5.99%	5.56%	5.26%	4.99%	5.49%	5.53%	5.65%	4.34%	4.04%
1.500	5.59%	5.87%	6.00%	6.19%	5.91%	6.05%	5.83%	5.98%	6.32%	5.91%	5.52%
1.750	4.50%	4.75%	5.25%	5.32%	5.28%	5.35%	5.29%	5.51%	5.48%	5.46%	5.59%
2.000	2.87%	3.30%	3.65%	3.57%	3.72%	3.70%	3.67%	3.96%	4.14%	4.25%	4.21%

Fortunately, the vast majority of holding period/SD pairs demonstrated a significant probability advantage, which provides compelling evidence of an option income strategy trading advantage. The preceding probability data is also invaluable as a guide for identifying, constructing, and managing an option income strategy with a proven historical probability advantage.

Option Income Strategy Back-Testing

For readers of my first book, the preceding background material should be familiar. Now that we have reviewed the foundation for how and why option income strategies work, it is time to explore new ground. The touch-probability framework above is still very useful, but there are limitations. The framework is heavily dependent on the accuracy of the calculation of the theoretical implied volatility of each hypothetical option. The volatility model I developed for this purpose incorporated the vertical (volatility as a function of strike price) and horizontal (volatility as a function of time to expiration) volatility skews. However, there will always be model errors relative to the actual implied volatilities derived from accurate market prices.

In addition to volatility model errors, the touch-probability analytical framework does not tell us when the price of the underlying security touched the short strike price, what the implied volatilities were at the time, what the prices of the options were, or how an actual, managed option income strategy would have performed in each period.

When I wrote my first book, the tools to answer the above questions did not exist, which is why I originally developed the touch-probability framework. Now, these tools do exist, which allowed me to evaluate the back-tested results of over 15,000 managed option income strategy trades for this article, each with identical, practicable entry and exit rules. Each trade was based on actual market prices and all trades included transaction costs.

To ensure consistent results, the identical option income strategy was used to generate all of the cumulative back-test results reported throughout this article. The next chapter will provide a detailed explanation of this option income strategy, including a comprehensive description of every objective entry and exit rule required to replicate these results. These same rules could also be used to trade the actual strategy in practice if so desired.

Finally, the aggregate performance metrics derived from all 15,000+ (unfiltered) trades will be reported, which will offer new insight into the profitability of option income strategies. Even more important, these metrics will serve as our benchmark for evaluating the performance of each of the trade filters presented in subsequent chapters.

2 - IRON CONDOR BACK-TEST

I used the iron condor strategy to generate all back-test results. The iron condor is arguably one of the purest, simplest, and most representative option income strategies, and one that explicitly exploits the chronic overvaluation of equity index options. Let's start with the basics. What is an iron condor and how is it constructed? It is the combination of two out-of-the-money (OTM) credit spreads: a bear call credit spread and a bull put credit spread.

We will review the out-of-the-money (OTM) bear call credit spread first. "Bear" means bearish, which indicates a strategy that performs well when the price of the underlying security declines. "Call" indicates the strategy is constructed using call options. "Spread" signifies that the strategy requires both the sale and purchase of a call option.

As I explained before, spreads are covered strategies that explicitly limit the maximum loss of the strategy to a fixed dollar amount that is known at the time the trade is entered. "Credit" spread indicates that the spread results in a cash inflow at the inception of the trade. This also means that we would be entitled to keep this cash inflow if the options we sold expired worthless (this explains the "income" in option income strategies). When originating a credit spread, we sell the option with the higher value and purchase the option of the same type (call or put) with the lower value. This is the source of the credit or inflow. For a call credit spread, we sell the option with the lower strike price and buy the option with the higher strike price.

Finally, the term "out-of-the-money" (OTM) tells us that the strike prices of the options used to construct the credit spread initially have no intrinsic value. In the case of OTM bear call credit spreads, OTM means that the strike prices of the call options are *above* the price of the underlying security when the trade is originated. We sell an OTM call option and buy a call option that is even farther

19

out of the money to limit our losses.

Figure 2.1 is a graphical representation of the payoff diagram for a generic OTM bear call credit spread. You will recall that the "payoff" to the option buyer is also called the intrinsic value and represents the value of exercising in-the-money (ITM) options at expiration. For every positive payoff received by an option buyer, there is a corresponding negative payoff incurred by an option seller.

Remember that the bear call credit spread requires the (short) sale and (long) purchase of an OTM call option. As explained above, the strike price of the long call option purchased will always be above (farther out-of-the-money than) the strike price of the short call option sold.

The payoff function of the OTM bear call credit spread in Figure 2.1 is depicted by three line segments. The first line segment is horizontal and begins at the left-side of the diagram and terminates at the strike price of the short call option. If the price of the underlying security was less than or equal to the strike price of the short call option at expiration, both call options would expire worthless. As a result, the value of the payoff function for the bull call credit spread equals zero for this entire region of the payoff function.

The next linear segment of the payoff function begins at the strike price of the short call option and ends at the strike price of the long call option (moving from left to right). In this region, the slope of the payoff function is negative 1.0 (per share). In other words, for every dollar the price of the underlying security increased in this region (at expiration), the payoff of the bear call credit spread strategy would *decrease* by one dollar (per share).

The third and final horizontal line segment at the right-side of the diagram depicts the payoff function for underlying security prices greater than the strike price of the long call option at expiration. Above this strike price of the *long* call option, the slope of the payoff function is zero. In this region of the payoff function, the short and long call option positions would both be in-the-money at expiration, so any *additional* increase in the price of the underlying security above the strike price of the long call option would not reduce our payoff any further.

When we execute an OTM bear call credit spread, we are a net seller of options. As you can see from the OTM bear call spread payoff diagram in Figure 2.1, the payoff value is always less than or

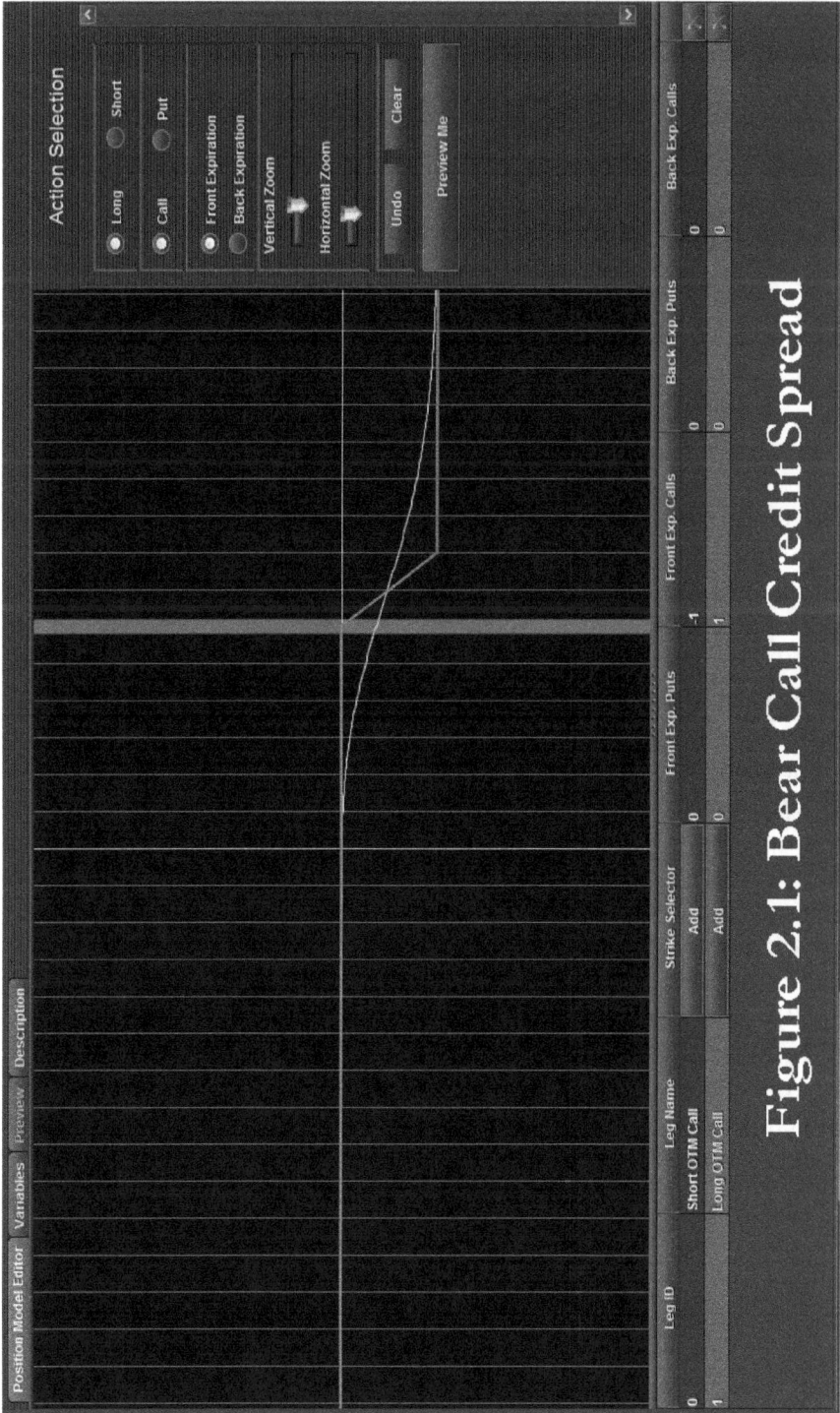

Figure 2.1: Bear Call Credit Spread

equal to zero. In exchange for accepting the risk of a negative future payoff, we demand a premium when we originate a credit spread trade. In equity index options, the magnitude of the average option premium has historically exceeded the average future payoff, which has generated excess returns for traders of option income strategies.

OTM Bull Put Credit Spread

Figure 2.2 is a graphical representation of the payoff diagram of a generic OTM bull put credit spread. "Bull" means bullish, which indicates a strategy that performs well when the price of the underlying security increases. "Put" indicates the strategy is constructed using put options, rather than call options.

However, in the case of OTM bull put credit spreads, OTM means that the strike prices of the put options are *below* the price of the underlying security when the trade is originated. The bull put credit spread requires the (short) sale and (long) purchase of an OTM put option. As explained above, when originating a credit spread, we sell the option with the higher value and purchase the option of the same type with the lower value. We sell an OTM put option and buy a put option that is even farther out of the money to limit our losses. As a result, the strike price of the long put option purchased will be below (farther out-of-the-money than) the strike price of the short put option sold.

The interpretation of the payoff diagram in Figure 2.2 is similar to the interpretation of Figure 2.1, with the same three corresponding payoff line segments. However, put payoff diagrams are intuitively easier to understand when evaluated from right-to-left (OTM to ITM). As was the case in the bear call credit spread example, the payoff (at expiration) for the bull put credit spread is always less than or equal to zero. We must receive compensation for this risk as well, which generates a second source of premium or income for the iron condor strategy.

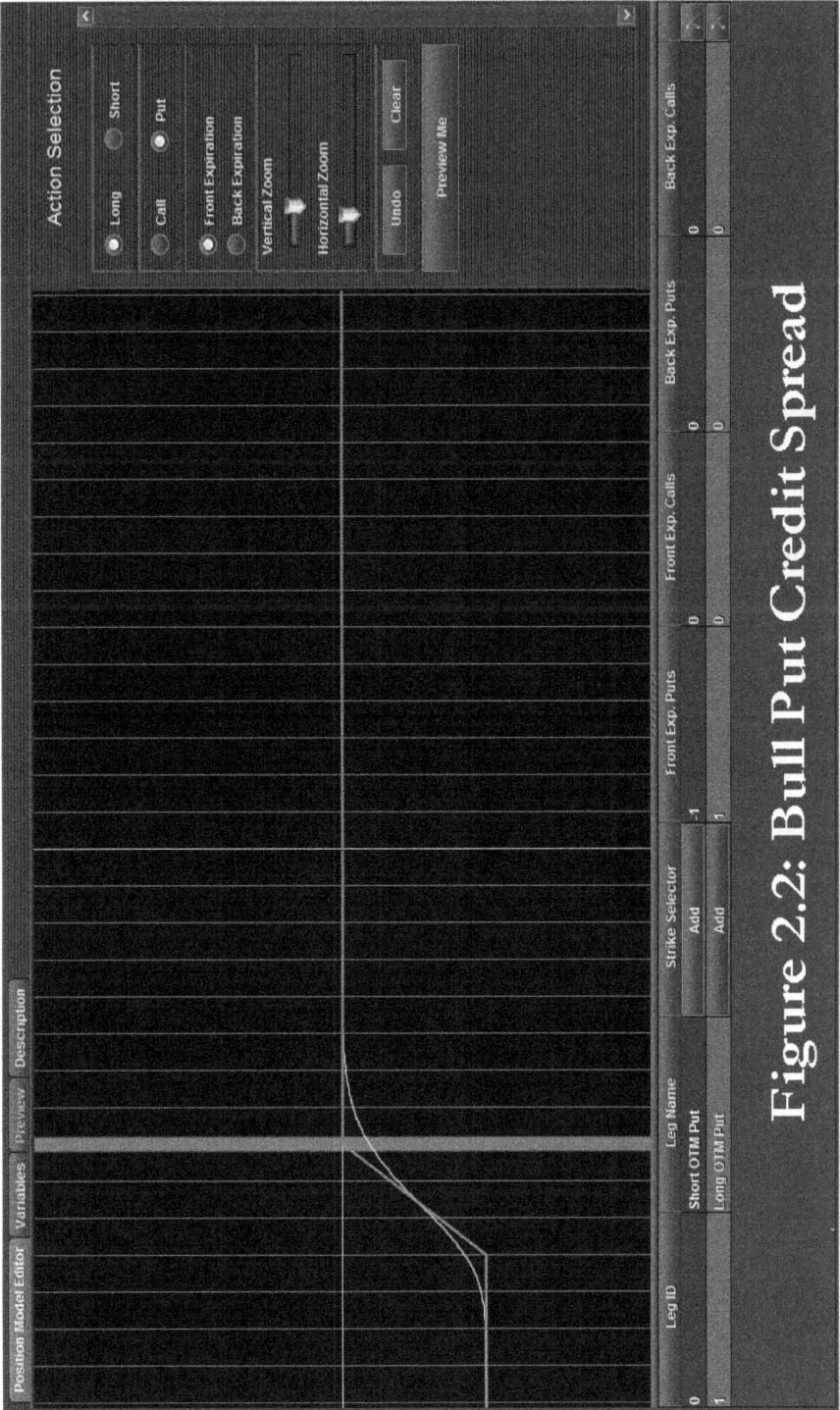

Figure 2.2: Bull Put Credit Spread

Iron Condor Strategy

The resulting iron condor strategy is the combination of an OTM bear call credit spread and an OTM bull put credit spread. Option income strategies are designed to be market neutral whenever possible and the iron condor is no exception. The "bear" and "bull" components cancel each other out, resulting in a strategy that experiences very little change in value in response to changes in the price of the underlying security – at least initially.

Figure 2.3 shows the payoff diagram for the iron condor strategy, which combines the payoff functions of the OTM bear call credit spread and OTM bull put credit spread into a single payoff function.

For underlying security prices below the strike price of the short put option at expiration (left side of diagram), the payoff is negative because the short put option expires in the money. Similarly, for underlying security prices above the strike price of the short call option at expiration (right side of diagram), the payoff is also negative because the short call option expires in the money. In the central region of the payoff function (between the strike prices of the short put and call options), the value of the payoff function equals zero because all options expire worthless.

This is our objective when implementing an iron condor strategy. We want all options to expire worthless. In general, if the realized price change of the underlying security is consistently less than the expected price change of the underlying security, the iron condor strategy will be profitable.

Asymmetric

You are probably asking yourself a few questions about Figure 2.3. Why does it appear to be asymmetric? Specifically, why is the OTM short put strike price located farther OTM (left) than the short call strike price (right)? And, why is the spread between the put strike prices wider than the spread between the call strike prices? The answer is the vertical volatility skew.

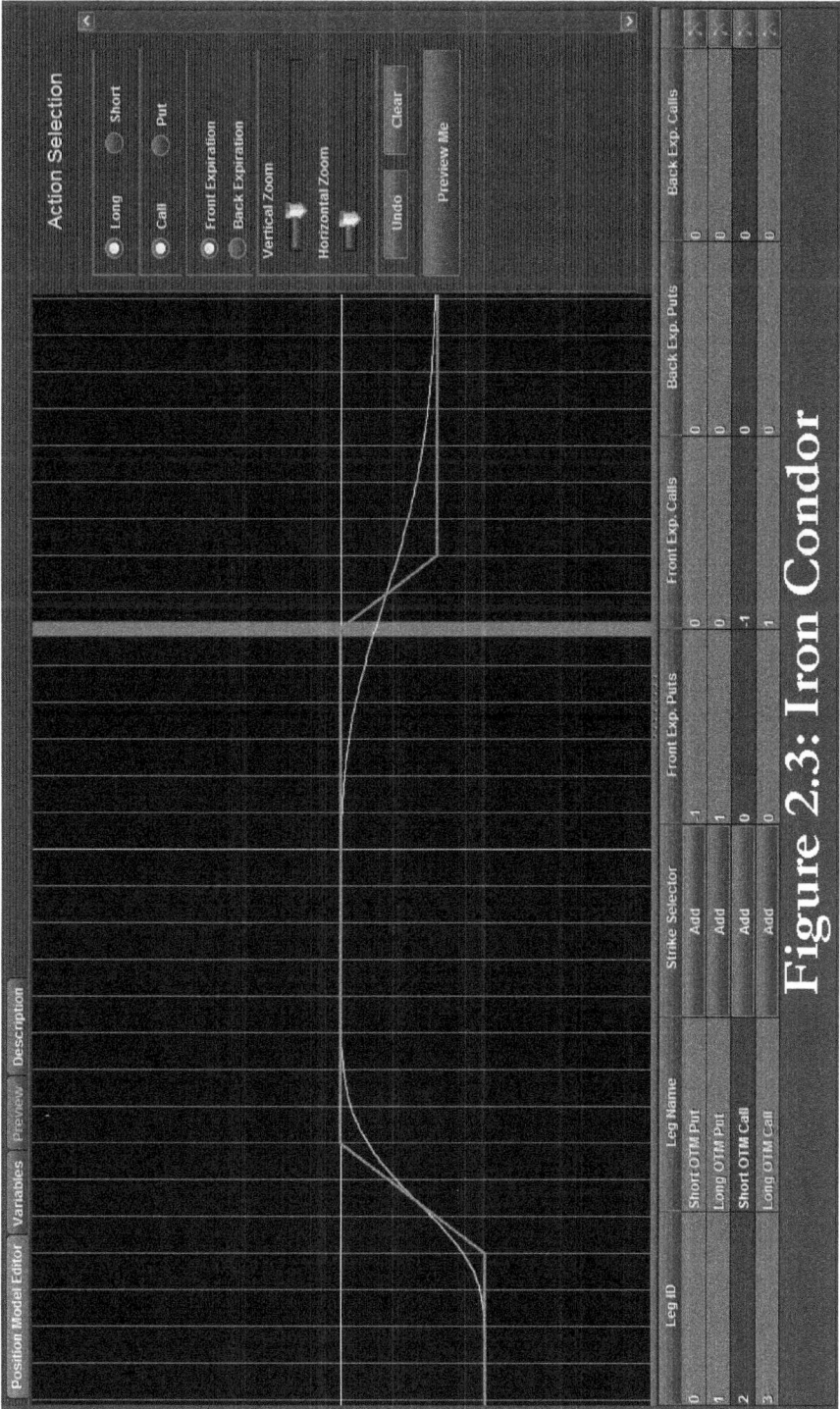

Figure 2.3: Iron Condor

Unfortunately, implied volatility is not constant across strike prices or expiration dates. Volatility modeling is beyond the scope of this article, but volatility skews are very important when selecting the appropriate strike prices and expiration dates for option income strategies. As a result, a brief introduction is required.

The Black-Scholes Option Pricing Model (BSOPM) assumes that volatility is constant and uniform, which is obviously not correct. Historically, equity prices have fallen much more rapidly than they have risen. As a result, equity options with lower strike prices have higher implied volatilities and equity options with higher strike prices have lower implied volatilities.

As a result, when attempting to determine the strike price of an OTM call option one standard deviation (SD) above the current market price, we would need to use a lower implied volatility than when calculating the strike price of an OTM put option one SD below the current market price. The resulting *plus one SD* strike price for the OTM call is closer to the current price of the underlying security than the *minus one SD* strike price for the OTM put. This is called the vertical skew and it answers all of the questions above.

It explains why the strike price of the short put option is farther OTM than the strike price of the short call option, and why the spread between the strike prices of the two put options is wider than the spread between the strike prices of the two call options. In equity index options, the implied volatility of OTM put options is higher than the implied volatility of OTM call options.

I used actual market prices and related derivatives (which incorporated the vertical skew) in the construction and back-testing of the iron condor strategy. This ensured that all of the iron condor trades were market-neutral and all back-test results were unbiased.

If you do not regularly work with the vertical skew and are more familiar with basic option models that ignore volatility skews, the asymmetric shape of the iron condor payoff diagram may seem strange. However, volatility skews are present in the actual market data and should always be integrated into your risk and return assumptions. Failure to incorporate volatility skews when constructing option strategies is one of the most common mistakes made by option traders.

External Resources

Before we delve further into the iron condor position model, trade rules and back-test procedures, I need to briefly describe the tools I used to do the strategy back-testing. This will help you understand the process that I used and how that process could be applied to other types of option strategies and back-tests.

The software that I used to conduct the back-tests is called QuantyCarlo, which was developed by Iota Technologies; many thanks to Larry Richards and Iota Technologies for their permission to include screen shots and back-test results from their software in this article. Figures 2.1 through 2.8 are all partial screen capture images from the QuantyCarlo software.

As I explained earlier, this technology which allows automated option strategy back-testing was not available until recently. I originally heard about QuantyCarlo through one of my readers and I was fortunate to be one of the first subscribers. QuantyCarlo subscriptions are not currently available from Iota, but may soon be available through OptionVue. For more information about discounts on qualifying OptionVue products and services, see the Resources Chapter at the end of this article.

Designing a user-friendly option strategy back-testing platform is a Herculean task. The sheer volume of data is enormous, with individual prices required for every option in the matrix. This means one call option price and one put option price for each strike price/expiration date combination. Adding intra-day data increases the amount of data by a factor of almost thirty. QuantyCarlo performs data integrity checks on the entire intra-day database to ensure the reliability of the strategy back-testing results.

While processing the volume of data is impressive, what makes QuantyCarlo powerful is its flexibility to calculate automated back-test results for almost any option strategy trade plan. It is limited only by the user's imagination – and by the user's ability to define the option strategy and trade rules in logical terms.

However, unlike most back-testing platforms, programming skills are not required. Every component of an option strategy and associated trade rules can be defined in QuantyCarlo by dragging and dropping individual elements and by selecting options from drop-down lists in the graphical user interface. The QuantyCarlo software automatically translates these user-friendly graphical depictions into a simple English-language translation, and into the source code required to conduct the back-test. No actual coding by the user is required.

An example of the user-interface can be seen on the right-side of figures 2.1, 2.2, and 2.3. I created the credit spreads in QuantyCarlo by clicking on: long or short, call or put, and front or back month. QuantyCarlo did the rest.

Designing a back-test in QuantyCarlo requires two main steps: 1) create a position model and 2) create a trade plan. A position model must objectively describe every option used to create the strategy and how many contracts of each option to buy or sell. The trade plan objectively describes when and how to enter, exit, and even adjust the strategy throughout the trade.

An example of the iron condor position model can be seen at the bottom of Figure 2.3. The first row specifies a short position of one put contract (-1) in the front month. The second row specifies a long position of one put contract (1), also in the front month. Together, these two positions make up the OTM bull put credit spread.

Similarly, the third row designates a short position of one call contract (-1) in the front month. The fourth row designates a long position of one call contract (1), again in the front month. Together, these two positions make up the OTM bear call credit spread. The entire four-leg position represents the iron condor position model.

However, you will note that we have not yet explicitly defined which strike price to use for each leg of the iron condor, which is why the "Add" button is shown in the strike selector column for each leg of the position model.

The remainder of this chapter will provide a detailed explanation of the iron condor position model and trade plan, including a comprehensive description of strike selectors and of every objective entry and exit rule used to produce the back-test results. Finally, the aggregate performance metrics derived from all 15,000+ (unfiltered) iron condor trades will also be reported.

QC Position Model – Strike Selection

Figure 2.3 illustrates all aspects of the iron condor position model, except for the strike selectors. In QuantyCarlo, there are many different ways to describe which strike price to select for each leg of a position model. One of the most intuitive and most useful strike selectors is Delta targets, which is what I used to create the iron condor position model.

Delta is the best known and most widely used "Greek" value. A comprehensive discussion of the Greeks is beyond the scope of this article. For a more comprehensive discussion, please refer to dedicated chapters on the Greeks in both of my earlier books (*Option Strategy Risk / Return Ratios* and *Exploiting Earnings Volatility*).

Briefly, Delta represents the change in the value of an option or option strategy for a small change in the price of the underlying security, holding all other variables constant. In other words, it is an instantaneous measure of price sensitivity, but it can also be used as an approximation or proxy for the probability of an option expiring in the money, which is very useful for strategy construction purposes.

This article contains very few formulas, but it is important to understand how and why Delta can be used as a proxy for the probability of an option expiring in the money. Please invest a few extra minutes to study the relationship I describe below. It will pay dividends when constructing your own option strategies.

Delta is actually a term in the Black-Scholes Option Pricing Model (BSOPM). The Delta of a call option (per share) equals N(d1) or the cumulative normal density function of the value d1, which is another term in the BSOPM that quantifies and normalizes the relationship between the strike price and the current price of the underlying security. As mentioned earlier, Delta (or N(d1)) is widely used and reported.

The terms d2 and N(d2) are also used in the BSOPM. N(d2) is *exactly* equal to the probability of an option expiring in the money. Unfortunately, N(d2) is not widely reported, which is why many traders use Delta (N(d1)) as a proxy for the probability of expiring in the money (N(d2)).

This is understandable because d2 equals d1, minus the quantity, sigma times the square root of the time remaining until expiration (in years). In this formula, sigma represents the annualized implied volatility, which is unique to each option. For short-term options in normal volatility environments, Delta is a reasonable proxy for the probability of expiring in the money. To gain some intuition on strategy construction, let's ignore the difference between Delta

(N(d1)) and the probability of expiring in the money (N(d2)) and focus on the practical use of Delta as a strike selector. So why is it useful to approximate the probability that each option will expire in the money (ITM)?

Estimating the ITM expiration probabilities allows us to accurately select individual strike prices among options with different implied volatilities. For example, if we wanted to position the short strikes of an iron condor exactly one standard deviation above (short call) and one standard deviation below (short put) the current price of an underlying security, we could use a normal probability table (or Excel NORMDIST function) to find the target Delta. From the NORMDIST function or probability table, we find that 0.16 represents the one-tail probability of an observation falling outside of one-standard deviation.

If we assume Delta is a reasonable proxy for the probability of an option expiring in the money, we would sell the call option with a per-share Delta of 0.16 and sell the put option with a per-share Delta of -0.16. While the Deltas are symmetric, the resulting strike prices of the OTM call and put options would not be symmetric. Why? Because of the asymmetric implied volatilities or vertical skew. This is the beauty of using Deltas to select strikes. Properly calculated, Delta automatically accounts for the differences in implied volatilities for every option in the matrix.

We are finally ready to review the actual Delta targets used to generate all of the iron condor back-test results. While I did not optimize the iron condor position model specifications or trade rules, I did rely on my trading experience and knowledge of option income strategies to design a practical and tradable iron condor strategy. I knew that it would take a lot of time and effort to generate and evaluate over 15,000 iron condor trades and I wanted to ensure that the results would be as meaningful and realistic as possible.

I could have used the above one-standard deviation (SD) Delta target of plus and minus 0.16 for the short strikes, but I knew there would be a better target value – even before running any back-tests on QuantyCarlo. Look back at the touch-probability advantages in Figures 1.5 and 1.6. The probability advantages were actually negative out to 0.75 standard deviations for OTM call options and only marginally positive for plus 1.0 standard deviation options.

In contrast, the touch-probabilities were consistently positive for

1.25 standard deviations for both OTM calls and puts. I could have gone farther out of the money than 1.25 standard deviations, but the size of average losses increases sharply relative to the size of average gains as we move farther out of the money. As a result, I selected a Delta target of plus and minus 0.11 for the short OTM call and put strikes of the iron condor strategy, which corresponds to 1.23 standard deviations above and below the current price of the underlying security.

For the long OTM calls and puts, I used a Delta target of plus and minus 0.08 respectively. I chose the Delta target of plus and minus 0.08 to ensure the resulting long and short strike prices would be different in all price and volatility environments.

On the date of every iron condor back-test trade entry, QuantyCarlo sold (short) the front-month OTM call and put options with per-share Deltas as close as possible to plus and minus 0.11 respectively.

Similarly, QuantyCarlo purchased (established long positions in) the front-month OTM call and put options with per-share Deltas as close as possible to plus and minus 0.08. The target Deltas of the long calls and puts were designed to offset, as were the target Deltas of the short calls and puts, resulting in approximately Delta-neutral iron condor trades.

QC Trade Plan

Now that we have thoroughly reviewed the iron condor position model, we can study the trade plan. You will recall that the trade plan objectively describes when and how to enter, exit, and adjust the strategy throughout the trade. Figure 2.4 is the QuantyCarlo trade plan screen for the iron condor strategy used to generate all of the back-test results in this article. You will notice sections for Pre-Entry Rules (collapsed), Entry Rules, Adjustment Rules (collapsed), and Exit Rules. In this case, the collapsed sections are empty. In other words, there are no pre-entry rules and no adjustment rules.

While adjustment rules are popular marketing tools for option strategy vendors, mentors, and advisors, adjustments are often counter-productive in option income strategies, resulting in excessive commissions and transaction costs. In fact, many adjustment techniques can entirely eliminate the inherent, probability-based trading edge of these strategies.

As a result, I did not include any adjustment rules in the iron condor trade plan. If you do plan to use adjustments in any option strategy, I would strongly encourage you to conduct a comprehensive back-test with and without the adjustments to understand how they impact the risk and return characteristics of the strategy.

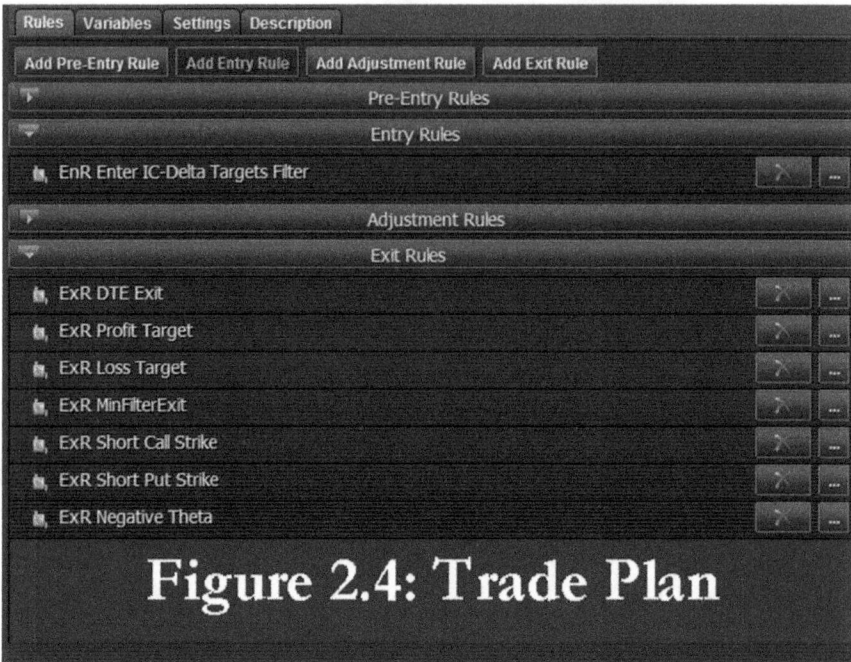

Figure 2.4: Trade Plan

While all of the trade rules are listed in Figure 2.4, we will review each of the individual trade rules in their respective Entry and Exit Rule sections that follow. For brevity, QuantyCarlo screen images will only be shown for the entry rule and for one of the exit rules. However, this should be sufficient to demonstrate how QuantyCarlo could be used to specify many different types of rules and conditions. All of the trade rules will be discussed in sufficient detail for the reader to replicate these results and to trade the back-tested iron condor strategy in practice.

QC Entry Rule

Figure 2.5 is a QC screen image of the Boolean condition that must be true to enter the iron condor trade. A Boolean condition is a fancy way of saying the condition is either true or false. When the Boolean condition is true or satisfied, a new iron condor trade is entered. When the condition is false, no trade occurs.

Let's look at the actual graphical Boolean entry rule at the top of the diagram. It may look a little complicated, but it is actually quite simple. The Boolean entry rule has three distinct elements, all of which must be true for the entry rule to be true.

The first element requires that the actual Days to Expiration (DTE) is less than or equal to the maximum days to expiration (Max DTE-IC) and the actual Days to Expiration (DTE) is also greater than or equal to the minimum days to expiration (Min DTE-IC). The maximum and minimum days to expiration are variables, with values that can be specified by the user when submitting the QC back-test.

If the minimum and maximum days to expiration were set to 50 and 75 respectively, a new iron condor would be entered whenever the actual number of calendar days to expiration was between 50 and 75 days, inclusive.

The second element of the Boolean condition is the PrepEntry Boolean variable. In this Boolean condition, I set all of the daily PrepEntry variable values to true. QuantyCarlo allows the user to upload actual true/false Boolean entry signals for every date, but I prefer to evaluate the daily entry conditions explicitly, which leads us to the third element of the Boolean condition.

The third element indicates that the "IC Score" must be greater than or equal to the minimum filter value (MinFilterValue). The MinFilterValue is also a user variable, with a value that can be entered by the user when submitting the back-test. In this case, the IC Score was calculated externally for every entry date and uploaded to QuantyCarlo. An iron condor trade is only entered when the IC Score for that specific date is greater than or equal to the minimum IC score, as specified by the user.

As mentioned earlier, the user drags and drops desired elements to create the graphical representation of the Boolean condition. QuantyCarlo creates the English-language representation, and the source code required to conduct the back-test.

This is a very simple, but powerful framework. Any external value or indicator can be uploaded and used in conjunction with specific user values or thresholds. The end result is an infinite array of custom filters that can be used to back-test targeted subsets of all historical iron condor trades.

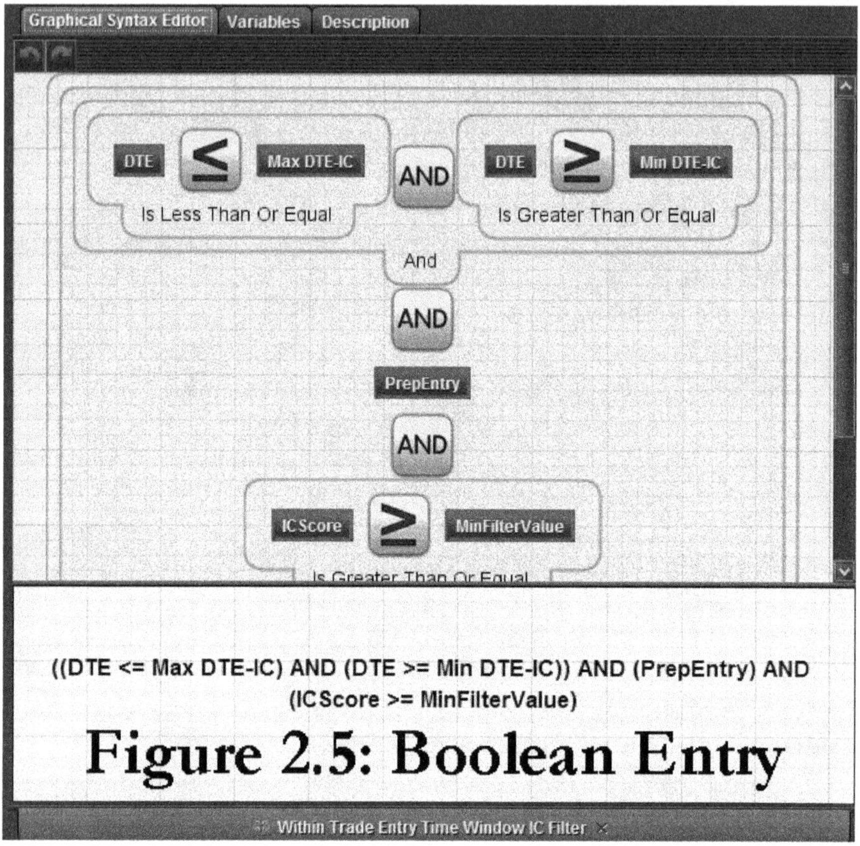

((DTE <= Max DTE-IC) AND (DTE >= Min DTE-IC)) AND (PrepEntry) AND (ICScore >= MinFilterValue)

Figure 2.5: Boolean Entry

So what happens when the preceding Boolean condition is true? The answer depends on the entry trade rule (Figure 2.6). In this case, when the Boolean condition on the left-side of Figure 2.6 is true, the trade rule performs three tasks. First, QuantyCarlo uses the position mode to enter the iron condor trade (AR Enter IC-Delta Targets).

The last two operations in the trade rule are optional. I assigned the initial margin (AX Assign Initial Margin) and initial yield (AX Assign Initial Yield) to individual variables, so that I could preserve these values for each trade entry to evaluate later.

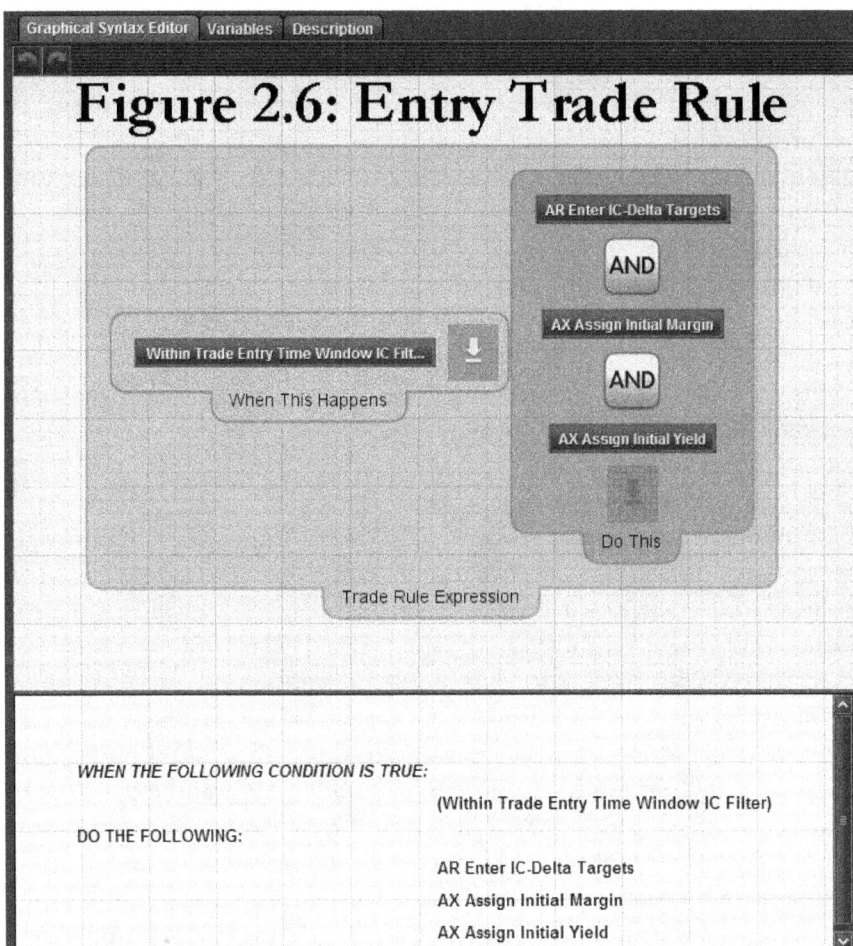

Figure 2.6: Entry Trade Rule

That's it. That is all that is required to define the trade entry. As was the case before, QuantyCarlo creates the English-language translation (bottom of Figure 2.6) and the source code (not shown) required to run the back-test.

The Back-Test Procedure

Before we examine the individual exit trade rules from the trade plan, let me explain the back-test procedure more fully, to ensure an accurate interpretation of the results provided throughout the remainder of this article.

The purpose of this article is to examine how filters can (and cannot) be used to enhance risk-adjusted returns of option income strategies. A secondary objective is to introduce some tools and techniques that will help you test and develop your own filters. In order to evaluate the effectiveness of each proposed filter, we need a baseline. In other words, we need to calculate aggregate performance metrics for all historical iron condor trades – without using any filters.

To do so, QuantyCarlo began with the entry rule described earlier. I set the minimum and maximum days until expiration to 25 and 75 respectively. Since I was interested in unfiltered trades, I set the minimum IC score to an extremely low value, which ensured execution of every iron condor trade that met the DTE entry requirements.

I ran the back-tests using end-of-day data on options with monthly expiration dates from May 2004 to May 2016. QuantyCarlo used the position model described earlier to generate daily iron condor trade entries on the S&P 500 Index (SPX), the Russell 2000 Index (RUT) and the NASDAQ 100 Index (NDX).

QuantyCarlo used the exit rules (described in the following sections) to manage each trade individually, which required checking each exit rule at the end of every trading day. I included transaction costs of $1.00 per contract, per leg, per trade (entry and exit). Due to occasional missing prices and other factors, some trade entries were "aborted," but the above back-tests still generated a total of 15,434 managed iron condor trades.

Finally, I exported the QuantyCarlo results for each of the 15,434 individual iron condor trades, scaled the results for each trade to a constant dollar amount at risk, applied an additional error-checking algorithm, and then calculated the aggregate performance metrics on the scaled and validated trade results.

In practice, we would obviously not enter a new iron condor trade every day on the SPX, RUT, and NDX, but we are not developing a trading strategy at this point; we are creating a performance benchmark to evaluate prospective trade filters. As a result, we are interested in understanding and evaluating the historical performance metrics derived from *every* iron condor trade, managed with a common and objective set of trade rules.

I could have evaluated the exit conditions every 15 minutes, instead of at the end of each trading day, but the time required to process over 15,000 managed trades at 15-minute intervals would have been excessive relative to the potential benefits. Using 15-minute intervals is much more practical when running a QC back-test on a sub-set of strategy transactions.

QC Exit Rules

Similar to QC entry rules, QC exit rules require a Boolean condition and the trade rule based on the condition. The Boolean condition for the first exit rule in the QC trade plan is depicted in Figure 2.7. It is very simple to understand. The Boolean condition is satisfied when the actual number of days to expiration (DTE) is less than or equal to the value of the user-specified DTE exit threshold variable (DTE Exit). I set the DTE Exit variable to *one day* for all iron condor strategy back-tests. If none of the exit rules were satisfied prior to expiration, the DTE Exit rule would force every iron condor trade to exit the at the close, exactly one calendar-day before option expiration.

For experienced iron condor traders, exiting only one day before expiration might seem extreme. Risk increases as time to expiration declines. However, as I explained earlier, I purposely did not optimize the iron condor trade rules; choosing a fixed number of days before expiration to exit the trade could have biased the results, due to extreme discrete events that occurred during the back-test period. That said, I *never* hold short option positions all the way to expiration, even covered option positions. It is a hard and fast rule. As a result, it would have been disingenuous of me to leave out the DTE exit rule entirely.

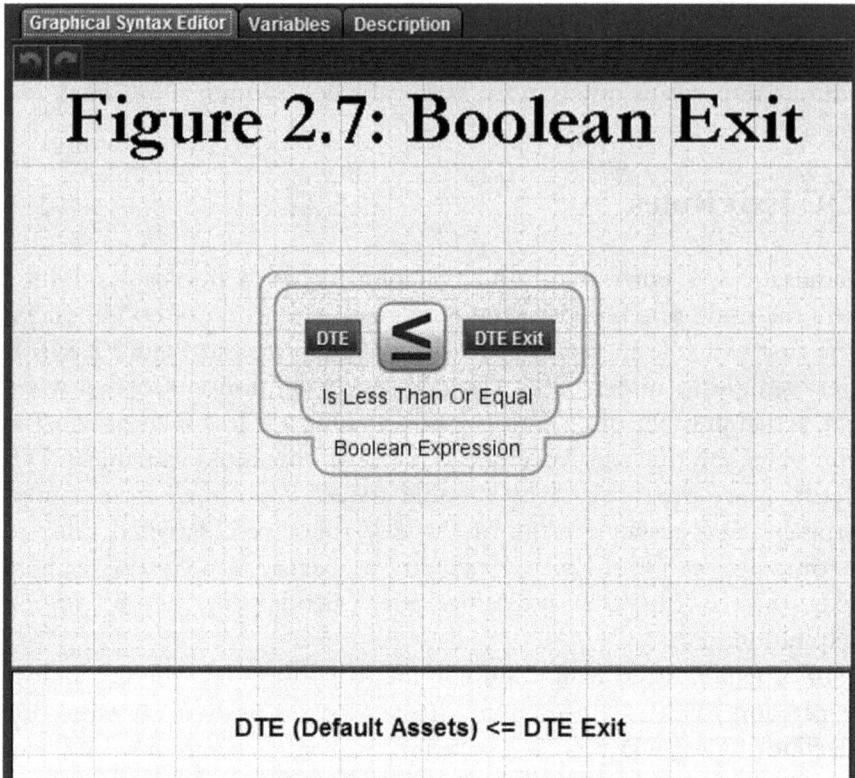

Figure 2.7: Boolean Exit

DTE ≤ DTE Exit

Is Less Than Or Equal

Boolean Expression

DTE (Default Assets) <= DTE Exit

As was the case with the entry rule, the exit trade rule determines what do to when the Boolean exit condition is satisfied. In this case, the exit trade rule shown in Figure 2.8 indicates that the iron condor trades were closed when the DTE Boolean exit condition (Figure 2.7) was satisfied.

Figure 2.8: Exit Trade Rule

Graphical Syntax Editor | Variables | Description

BN DTE Exit

When This Happens

Close Trade

Do This

Trade Rule Expression

WHEN THE FOLLOWING CONDITION IS TRUE:

(BN DTE Exit)

DO THE FOLLOWING:

Close Trade (Default Assets)

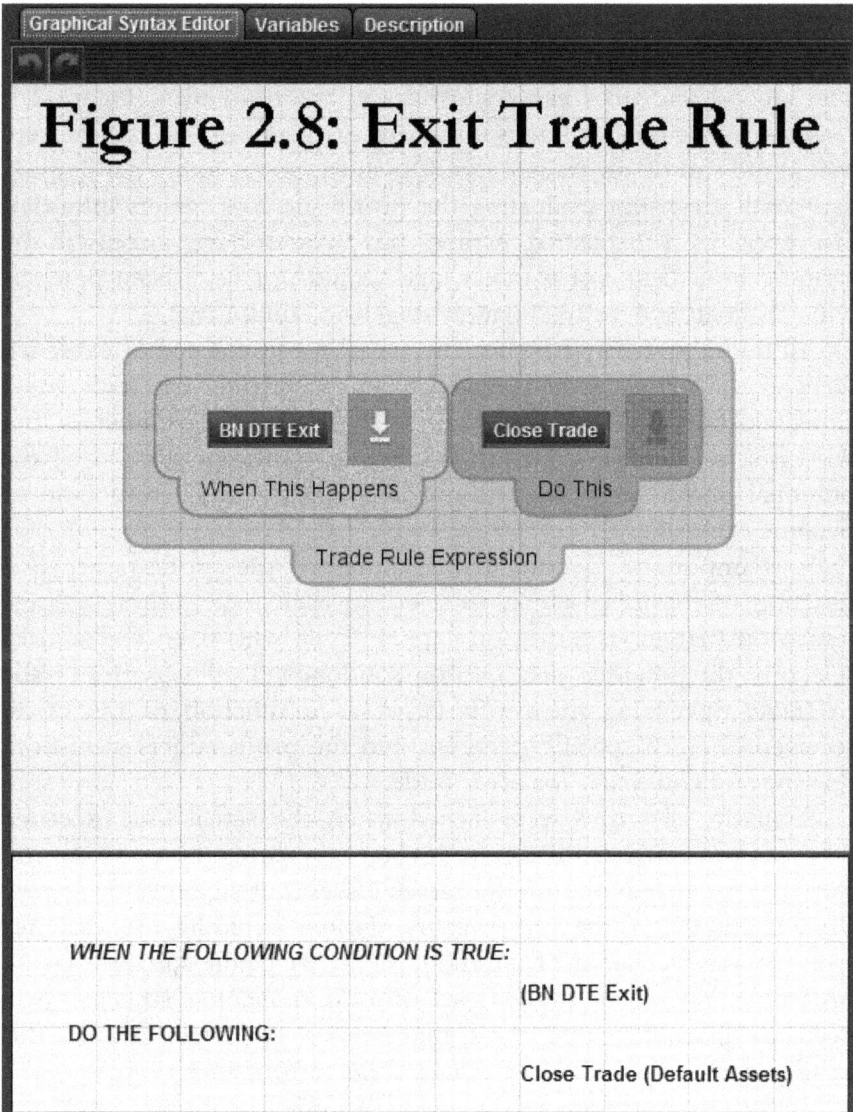

Remaining Exit Rules

In addition to the DTE exit rule described above, there are six additional exit rules listed in the Figure 2.4 trade plan. Each of these trade rules will be discussed individually, followed by a summary of the unfiltered iron condor strategy results at the end of this chapter.

Profit and Loss Targets

The second and third exit trade rules in the trade plan (Figure 2.4) closed the iron condor trades if the strategy profit or loss targets were met at the end of any trading day. Obviously some additional slippage can result from not evaluating the profit and loss targets intra-day. However, as I explained earlier, this would have increased the runtime by a factor of thirty, which would not have been practical when evaluating over 15,000 individual iron condor trades.

All trades were closed when the actual profit equaled or exceeded 90% of the initial credit received when originating the trade. As I explained before, I did not optimize the trade rule parameters, but 90% is a reasonable value. It captures a significant portion of the potential option premium without allowing the risk-return ratio to become excessive.

It is important to note that I expressed the profit target as a function of the initial credit received on each trade, not as a target return on margin or return on capital. Even with fixed Delta strike selectors, the potential yield on iron condors will still vary from trade to trade. Specifying the profit target as a function of the credit received on each specific trade ensured the profit targets were both realistic and consistent for every trade.

Similarly, all trades were closed when the actual loss exceeded 200% of the initial credit received when originating the trade. As you can see, the magnitude of the target losses will significantly exceed the magnitude of the target gains. This is typically the case for strategies that sell out-of-the-money (OTM) credit spreads. To be profitable long-term, these types of option income strategies will need to generate more wins than losses. We will explore this relationship further when we evaluate the performance results.

Before we move on, let's go through a quick profit and loss target example. If we received a credit of $5,000 upon originating a specific iron condor trade, the above exit rules would close that specific trade if the end-of-day profit equaled or exceeded $4,500 ($5,000 * 0.90) or the magnitude of the end-of-day loss equaled or exceeded $10,000 ($5,000 * 2.00).

Unfavorable Trading Environments

In addition to closing trades when specific profit and loss targets are met, we can also close trades when the risk-characteristics of the trades become unfavorable. One way to identify these types of hostile environments is to use price targets for the underlying stock. As we move closer to the upper and lower negative payoff regions of the iron condor payoff diagram (Figure 2.3), risk increases and return decreases. As a result, many option traders choose to exit credit spread trades when the price of the underlying security reaches or "touches" the short strike price.

This should remind you of the "touch-probabilities" that we reviewed earlier. We used the touch-probability calculations to identify a reasonable Delta target for the strike prices of the short put and call options. Setting the underlying exit price targets equal to the short strike prices is perfectly consistent with the touch-probability research.

The fifth and sixth exit rules in Figure 2.4 were used to implement these exit conditions. All trades were closed if the price of the underlying security was greater than or equal to the strike price of the short call option or less than or equal to the strike price of the short put option. As was the case earlier, both of these exit conditions were evaluated at each day's close, not intra-day. You will note that I did not address the fourth exit rule in Figure 2.4 ("ExR MinFilterExit"). It was not used to generate the unfiltered performance results, but we will review this rule when applicable.

I used one final exit rule to close iron condor trades when they entered unfavorable trading environments. If the Theta of the iron condor position was negative at the end of any trading day, the trade was closed. As you will recall, Theta represents the change in the value of an option or option strategy as a function of the passage of time. By definition, Theta is positive for all option income strategies – at least initially.

Theta represents our compensation for accepting the risk of an option income strategy. However, Theta is not constant and will change in response to evolving market conditions. If Theta becomes negative, the iron condor would no longer be considered an option income strategy and should be closed. The negative Theta exit rule is applicable to all option income strategies.

Trade Plan Summary

That's it. That completes our review of the QC entry and exit rules used to generate all 15,434 iron condor trades. The trades were entered daily with 25 to 75 calendar days remaining until expiration. Trades were closed at the end of the day upon reaching a profit target of 90% of the initial credit or a loss target of 200% of the initial credit. Trades were also closed if the closing price of the underlying stock touched the strike prices of the short call or put options. If none of the above exit conditions were met during the life of the trade, the trade was closed one day prior to option expiration.

Unfiltered Iron Condor Results

Using the QC trade plan in conjunction with the scaling and validation process described earlier, I calculated three different summary performance metrics on the resulting 15,434 managed iron condor trades. The first metric I calculated was profit factor. Profit factor represents the gains earned per dollar of losses incurred. Profitable strategies have profit factors above 1.0 and unprofitable strategies have profit factors below 1.0. Profit factors are positive by definition.

Profit factor is a function of the percentage of wins relative to the percentage of losses, and the average magnitude of those wins relative to the average magnitude of those losses. The resulting profit factor represents the cumulative gains divided by the cumulative losses. For those mathematically inclined, the formulas below will provide some further insight into profit factor. Note that all of the values in the formulas below are positive. In other words, both profits and losses are expressed as positive numbers.

Profit Factor =   **(% of Wins / % of Losses) ***
                                   (Average Win / Average Loss)

Profit Factor = (Cumulative Wins / Cumulative Losses)

As shown in Figure 2.9, the unfiltered managed iron condor trading strategy had a profit factor of 2.10 from May 2004 to May 2016. The "1TPS" in the heading indicates one trade per signal, which in this case represents a new iron condor trade every day on the RUT, SPX, and NDX.

The other two performance metrics are even easier to understand. The percentage of winning trades was 85.10% and the average return on margin was 3.22%. The average return on margin includes both winning and losing trades.

Margin represents the maximum possible loss incurred on each trade, which also corresponds to the amount of capital required to implement the trade. Since we can only incur the negative payoff on one side of the trade at expiration, the amount of margin or capital required will equal the maximum adverse payout, less the total credit generated on the trade. If you would like to review the iron condor payoff function, please revisit Figure 2.3.

Figure 2.9: 1TPS - No Filter IC (RUT, SPX, NDX)

Filter Condition	Profit Factor	% Winning Trades	Avg. Return on Margin	% of Total Trades
None (ALL Trades)	2.10	85.10%	3.22%	100.00%

The ratio of winning to losing trades is not provided in Figure 2.9, but you could use the profit factor formula to solve for this value. As you can see in the derivation below, the average loss was 2.72 times the size of the average win. As explained earlier, this is a direct result of selling OTM credit spreads.

Profit Factor = (% of Wins / % of Losses) * (Average Win / Average Loss)

2.10 = (85.10% / 14.9%) * (Average Win / Average Loss)

Average Win / Average Loss = 2.10 / (85.10% / 14.9%)

Average Win / Average Loss = 2.10 / (5.7114)

Average Win / Average Loss = 0.36769 or 1/2.72

The final column above represents the percentage of total trades used to generate the reported results. Since the strategy results were not filtered, 100% or all 15,434 trades were included in the performance metric calculations. The percentage of total trades will be more relevant when we examine the filtered results. The filtered percentages of total trades will reveal the percentage of all trades that met the filter criteria at trade inception.

You may be asking why we are only examining the results of iron condors using monthly (rather than weekly) options. The unfiltered trade results from a managed *weekly* iron condor strategy are presented in Figure 2.10. The same trade plan was used, except the minimum and maximum days to expiration (DTE) were 4 and 17 respectively. I used the same process to export, scale, and validate the trade results. The performance metric calculations were also the same.

Figure 2.10: 1TPS - No Filter IC Weekly (RUT, SPX, NDX)				
Filter Condition	Profit Factor	% Winning Trades	Avg. Return on Margin	% of Total Trades
None (ALL Trades)	1.39	81.46%	1.28%	100.00%

As you can see from Figure 2.10, the performance of the weekly iron condor was much worse than the performance of the monthly iron condor. The weekly iron condor strategy was still profitable, but not nearly as lucrative as the monthly strategy. It is beyond the scope of this article to fully examine the sources of the performance differences, but keep in mind that monthly options are a more efficient hedging vehicle. The demand for options as a hedging (risk reduction) vehicle is one of the principal underlying factors responsible for the chronic overvaluation of equity index options, which could partially explain the performance differences between monthly and weekly iron condor strategies.

The monthly profit factor (2.10 versus 1.39), percentage of winning trades (85.10% versus 81.46%) and average return on margin (3.22% versus 1.28%) dominate the performance metrics of the weekly strategy. As a result, the remainder of the article focuses exclusively on monthly iron condor strategies.

The aggregate monthly results are impressive, especially for a non-optimized, unfiltered iron condor strategy that included transaction costs. The performance metrics were derived from an objective, practical trading strategy (trade plan) that used actual option prices to generate over 15,000 trades over a 12-year period. This provides compelling evidence on the profitability of option income strategies, but we can do even better with the right type of trade filters.

3 - TREND FILTERS

In the next few chapters, we will review the iron condor strategy performance metrics for various filtered subsets of the 15,000+ trades generated by QuantyCarlo. In this chapter, we will begin to examine how applying different types of trend filters affected the performance metrics of the managed iron condor strategy. For each trend filter, we will evaluate the results for a range of parameter values.

Before we analyze the results, let's briefly review favorable and unfavorable environments for the iron condor. As you will recall from Chapter 2, an iron condor is the combination of two credit spreads and has a payoff function that is always less than or equal to zero. As a result, we know that the iron condor strategy must be a net seller of options. Ideally, all options would expire worthless, which would result in a zero payoff. In our managed iron condor strategy, we would like to reach our profit target before the price of the underlying security touches the strike prices of either the short put or short call option, and before the maximum loss trigger is reached.

This happens when the *realized* price movement of the underlying security is less than the *expected* price movement that was embedded in the price of the options when the trade was initiated. Said differently, the iron condor strategy performs well when the *realized* volatility during the life of a specific trade is less than the initial *implied* volatility. It is important to remember that the iron condor strategy will perform poorly when the price of the underlying security *moves up or down* faster or farther than anticipated.

That said, most experienced traders have vivid and painful memories of owning iron condors during market panics that caused wild volatility spikes and plummeting prices. We may not recall as readily the iron condor losses incurred during sleepy markets that grinded higher day after day, but many such losses did occur. Death by a thousand cuts and a stake through the heart both yield the same result.

While iron condor losses can occur from both upward and downward price movements, there is an asymmetric volatility component to consider as well. As you will recall from Chapter 2, the vertical volatility skew in equity index options will result in our iron condor having a larger negative payoff to the downside than to the upside (Figure 2.3). In addition, when equity prices decline, realized and implied volatility both tend to increase. Iron condors have a negative Vega, which means they perform poorly when implied volatility increases. As a result, our iron condor strategy may perform worse in down versus up markets. All of these elements are important to consider when evaluating the performance of trade filters and *especially the logic behind them.*

Moving Average Price Filters

The first step in developing a trading strategy is to begin with a market-edge hypothesis that we hope to test and validate through our back-test. Ideally, the hypothesis should be based on years of research and practical trading experience. Such experience helps traders understand how and why markets move and should continually be focused on identifying market anomalies that could be exploited to generate excess risk-adjusted returns.

With respect to trend filters, one plausible hypothesis is that there are long-term trends in the equity markets that are a function of cyclical economic environments. Trend-following strategies are one of the longest-running professional trading strategies and there is extensive evidence that these strategies have proven to be successful across a wide range of trading instruments, including equities.

While the iron condor is a market-neutral strategy, rapid downward price moves accompanied by extreme volatility spikes are very painful for iron condor traders. If these types of dramatic down-moves occur less frequently when prices are moving higher, then it would be reasonable to assume the iron condor strategy would perform better in up-trending markets.

One of the easiest and simplest ways to define an up-trend is with a simple moving average. If the price of the underlying security is above its moving average, the market would be in an uptrend and vice versa. If these environments eliminate some of the worst performing iron condor trades, the iron condor performance metrics in filtered up-trending environments should be better than the unfiltered iron condor performance metrics – at least according to our hypothesis.

Figure 3.1 presents the performance metrics for the simple moving average price filter. The first row repeats the aggregate results for the 15,434 unfiltered iron condor trades, followed by the performance metrics for nine different trend-filtered strategies with parameter values ranging from 50 days to 250 days. The same performance metrics will be used to evaluate all strategy results: profit factor, percentage of winning trades, average return on margin, and percentage of total trades.

The 250-day moving average price filter arguably generated the best results. It had the highest profit factor (2.20) and highest percentage of winning trades (85.81%), but these values were only marginally higher than the unfiltered profit factor (2.10) and percentage of winning trades (85.10%). Even with the higher profit factor and higher percentage of winning trades, the average return on margin was slightly *lower* than the unfiltered trades (3.19% versus 3.22%). Even if we adopted this filter, we would be excluding 25% of our trading opportunities for a very marginal improvement in the profit factor and in the percentage of winning trades. Surprisingly, many of the moving average price filters performed even *worse* than the unfiltered iron condor strategy.

Figure 3.1: 1TPS - MA Price Filter (RUT, SPX, NDX)					
Price Condition	Moving Average Period	Profit Factor	% Winning Trades	Avg. Return on Margin	% of Total Trades
N/A (ALL)	N/A (ALL)	2.10	85.10%	3.22%	100.00%
Price >= MA	50	1.96	84.14%	2.83%	63.81%
Price >= MA	75	2.07	84.66%	3.00%	65.80%
Price >= MA	100	2.04	84.56%	2.95%	67.57%
Price >= MA	125	2.05	84.70%	2.96%	69.50%
Price >= MA	150	2.10	85.05%	3.03%	70.97%
Price >= MA	175	2.11	85.23%	3.05%	71.79%
Price >= MA	200	2.12	85.43%	3.08%	73.00%
Price >= MA	225	2.18	85.72%	3.16%	73.47%
Price >= MA	250	2.20	85.81%	3.19%	75.12%

What conclusion can we draw from the above data? Even with a well-reasoned market hypothesis, there is no guarantee that our proposed filters will yield excess returns historically, let alone in the future.

Moving Average Volatility Filters

We already know that volatility and price are negatively correlated in the equity market. As a result, we can construct a similar market-edge hypothesis using moving average *volatility* filters. If dramatic price declines occur less frequently when volatility is moving *lower*, then it would be reasonable to assume the iron condor strategy would perform better when implied volatility is trending *lower*.

Figure 3.2 presents the performance metrics for the simple moving average volatility filter. The first row repeats the aggregate results for the 15,434 unfiltered iron condor trades, followed by the performance metrics for nine different trend-filtered strategies with parameter values ranging from 50 days to 250 days.

Figure 3.2: 1TPS - MA IV Filter (RUT, SPX, NDX)					
Implied Volatility Index Condition	Moving Average Period	Profit Factor	% Winning Trades	Avg. Return on Margin	% of Total Trades
N/A (ALL)	N/A (ALL)	2.10	85.10%	3.22%	100.00%
IV <= MA	50	1.97	84.12%	2.92%	60.06%
IV <= MA	75	1.99	84.25%	2.95%	60.98%
IV <= MA	100	1.93	83.96%	2.83%	60.55%
IV <= MA	125	2.00	84.30%	2.94%	60.72%
IV <= MA	150	2.12	84.97%	3.12%	60.28%
IV <= MA	175	2.18	85.28%	3.20%	60.35%
IV <= MA	200	2.20	85.48%	3.22%	60.65%
IV <= MA	225	2.19	85.47%	3.20%	61.01%
IV <= MA	250	2.13	85.19%	3.10%	61.22%

The 200-day moving average volatility filter arguably generated the best results. It had the highest profit factor (2.20) and highest percentage of winning trades (85.48%), but as was the case with the best moving average price filter, these values were only marginally higher than the unfiltered profit factor (2.10) and unfiltered percentage of winning trades (85.10%). The average return on margin was exactly the same as the unfiltered trades (3.22%) and most of the other moving average volatility filters performed *worse* than the unfiltered iron condor strategy.

DMI Price Filters

Perhaps simple moving average filters are just too simple. Another well-known directional indicator is J. Wells Wilder Jr.'s Directional Movement Indicator (DMI) that he introduced in his ground-breaking 1978 book *New Concepts in Technical Trading Systems.* According to Wilder,

"Directional movement is the most fascinating concept I have studied. Defining it is a little like chasing the end of a rainbow...Certainly one of my most satisfying achievements was the day I was actually able to reduce this concept to an absolute mathematical equation." Unlike moving averages, Wilder's DMI is a function of each day's directional movement, which he defines as the *"largest part of today's range that is outside of yesterday's range."* Wilder volatility-adjusts each period's directional movement and calculates the cumulative directional movement over a given number of periods. Positive DMI values indicate uptrends and negative DMI values indicate downtrends for the specified period.

Our market-edge hypothesis would suggest that iron condors should perform better in up-trending markets, or when DMI is greater than zero. Figure 3.3 shows the performance metrics for the DMI filter. The first row repeats the aggregate results for the 15,434 unfiltered iron condor trades, followed by the performance metrics for nine different DMI-filtered strategies with parameter values ranging from 50 trading days to 250 trading days.

The 50-day DMI filter generated the best results in two out of the three performance metrics. It had the highest profit factor (2.25), the highest average return on margin (3.26%), but only the fourth-highest percentage of winning trades (85.36%). The 50-day DMI performance metrics were only marginally higher than the unfiltered profit factor (2.10), average return on margin (3.22%), and unfiltered percentage of winning trades (85.10%). As was the case for the other two trend filters, most of the other DMI filters performed *worse* than the unfiltered iron condor strategy.

Figure 3.3: 1TPS - DMI Filter (RUT, SPX, NDX)					
DMI Condition	DMI Period	Profit Factor	% Winning Trades	Avg. Return on Margin	% of Total Trades
N/A (ALL)	N/A (ALL)	2.10	85.10%	3.22%	100.00%
DMI > 0	50	2.25	85.36%	3.26%	47.93%
DMI > 0	75	2.01	84.30%	2.89%	48.57%
DMI > 0	100	2.24	85.77%	3.23%	48.04%
DMI > 0	125	2.23	85.90%	3.21%	49.55%
DMI > 0	150	2.16	85.44%	3.09%	48.80%
DMI > 0	175	2.02	84.67%	2.87%	48.70%
DMI > 0	200	2.04	84.87%	2.89%	48.04%
DMI > 0	225	1.99	84.41%	2.82%	48.24%
DMI > 0	250	1.89	83.78%	2.65%	48.17%

Despite a credible market-edge hypothesis, the trend-filtered results were obviously not very encouraging. As you can see from the data, it is very challenging to develop a credible market-edge hypothesis and analogous trade filter that significantly enhances the risk-adjusted returns of option income strategies. If you have developed your own rule-based trading strategies, this will be no surprise. Fortunately, there is a different type of trade filter that shows more promise: what I call the *discriminating* filter.

4 - DISCRIMINATING FILTERS

Discriminating filters are very different from the trend filters presented in Chapter 3. Unlike trend filters, discriminating filters exclude an increasing percentage of trades as the filter condition or threshold becomes more extreme or restrictive. If we can develop a credible market-edge hypothesis using discriminating filters, we should be able to consistently identify the best possible option-income trades.

Given the importance of the discriminating filter concept, let's review a simple example before we continue. Directional strategies are more intuitive than market-neutral strategies, so I will use a simple bullish directional strategy as the foundation for the discriminating filter example. One of the most robust directional strategies involves buying equities after they have declined in price, but are still in long-term uptrends. The corresponding market-edge hypothesis would suggest that equity indices are more attractively priced after pullbacks and prices should eventually continue in the direction of the long-term uptrend as the economy and earnings continue their cyclical growth pattern. After such pullbacks, we would expect long equity index trades to generate attractive risk-adjusted returns.

To define the long-term uptrend, we could use a simple moving average filter, such as requiring the closing price to be greater than or equal to the 100-day, 150-day, or 200-day moving average. Now that we have a systematic means of identifying uptrends, we need to determine which trades to enter. If we expect the uptrend to continue, it would be logical to assume that larger pullbacks would generate higher future returns for our long-only or bullish equity index strategy. We can use this assumed relationship to create a discriminating filter.

In this example, the discriminating filter value could represent the percentage decline in the equity price from the recent peak. If our market-edge hypothesis is valid, we should see improving performance metrics that are a direct function of the magnitude of the pullback. In other words, long (buy) trades entered after 5% declines should perform better than long trades entered after 4% declines, which should perform better than long trades entered after 3% declines, and so on.

The performance metrics should be highly correlated with the filter threshold and the performance metrics should all improve as the filter threshold becomes more restrictive (larger percentage pullbacks). As we make the threshold values increasingly restrictive (larger required pullback), fewer trades should qualify, but they should generate a higher profit factor, better return on margin and a higher percentage of winning trades. I included this simplistic example of a discriminating filter for demonstration purposes only; however, I encourage you to back-test these types of directional option trade strategies using a wide range of discriminating filters. Bullish pullback strategies can offer attractive risk-adjusted returns and would complement your non-directional option income strategies.

CBOE SKEW Filter

The Black Scholes Option Pricing Model (BSOPM) is a remarkable tool, but every one of its underlying assumptions is violated in practice. Particularly relevant: returns are not distributed log-normally. As I explained in Chapter 2, equity prices have historically fallen much more rapidly than they have risen. Since the market crash of 1987, traders have recognized *"that S&P 500 tail risk - the risk of outlier returns two or more standard deviations below the mean - is significantly greater than under a lognormal distribution.* In response, the CBOE created the SKEW index to quantify the degree that expected returns deviate from the log-normal distribution.

"The CBOE SKEW Index ("SKEW") is an index derived from the price of S&P 500 tail risk. Similar to VIX®, the price of S&P 500 tail risk is calculated from the prices of S&P 500 out-of-the-money options. SKEW typically ranges from 100 to 150. A SKEW value of 100 means that the perceived distribution of S&P 500 log-returns is normal, and the probability of outlier returns is therefore negligible. As SKEW rises above 100, the left tail of

the S&P 500 distribution acquires more weight, and the probabilities of outlier returns become more significant. Since an increase in perceived tail risk increases the relative demand for low strike puts, increases in SKEW also correspond to an overall steepening of the curve of implied volatilities, familiar to option traders as the skew."

The above CBOE description provides an excellent introduction to the CBOE SKEW index. For traders who would like a more detailed explanation, the CBOE also provides a white paper on their website that describes the mechanics of the SKEW index calculations.

Before we attempt to develop a market-edge hypothesis based on the SKEW, let's examine how the SKEW index behaves in practice. Figure 4.1 shows the daily correlation from 2000 to September 2016 between pairs of thee variables: the SKEW index, the VIX index, and the SPX (S&P 500 index). Correlation is a measure of the strength of the linear relationship between two variables. Correlation values range from negative one to positive one. Negatively correlated variables tend to move in opposite directions and positively correlated variables tend to move in the same direction. Obviously, every variable is perfectly positively correlated with itself (correlation = + 1.0)

As we have already discussed, the price of SPX and the implied volatility of SPX options (measured by the VIX index) are negatively correlated (-0.498) and tend to move in opposite directions (Figure 4.1). As the price of SPX increases, the implied volatilities of SPX options decline. Prolonged periods of SPX price increases and declining implied volatilities can make SPX investors apprehensive about a possible market correction. Fortunately, the decline in implied volatilities creates an opportunity to hedge their long positions inexpensively. The resulting increased demand for OTM put options forces OTM put option prices and their implied volatilities to increase. This raises the implicit probability of tail risk and results in an increase in the SKEW index. As a result, the SKEW index is positively correlated with SPX prices (+0.583) and negatively correlated with the VIX index (-0.355).

Figure 4.1: Correlation (SKEW, SPX, VIX)			
2000 - 9/2016	*SKEW*	*VIX*	*SPX*
SKEW	1		
VIX	-0.355	1	
SPX	0.583	-0.498	1

The key challenge is to develop a market-edge hypothesis and discriminating filter based on the behavior of OTM put option buyers and the resulting changes in the SKEW index. To accomplish this objective, we need to know whether the SPX hedgers should be considered the "smart-money" or "dumb-money." In other words, do we bet with them or against them?

In my experience developing, testing, and trading directional strategies, I have noted that SKEW index values above 130 are often followed by poor equity performance and unusually large price declines. This is the worst possible environment for our iron condor strategy.

Based on the above market-edge hypothesis, we can use the SKEW index to create a discriminating filter, only entering iron condor trades when the SKEW index is less than or equal to a given threshold value, 130 for example. If the market-edge hypothesis is valid, the performance metrics should be negatively correlated with the SKEW index threshold. In other words, as we accept trades in environments with higher and higher SKEW index values, the performance of the iron condor strategy should suffer. Similarly, as we reduce the SKEW index threshold, the performance metrics should continually improve. If you are an experienced option trader with knowledge of the SKEW index, take a moment and create your own market-edge hypothesis before reviewing the SKEW filter results.

So was my premise confirmed by the historical data? I initially hypothesized that accepting trades when the SKEW index was less than or equal to 130 should generate superior performance results. As evidenced in Figure 4.2, the resulting profit factor of 2.27 exceeded the profit factor for all unfiltered trades (2.10). The percentage of winning trades increased from 85.10% to 86.24%, and the average return on margin increased from 3.22% to 3.52%. So far

– so good.

However, the correlation between the SKEW threshold and the percentage of winning trades and average return on margin were 0.736 and 0.701 respectively (Figure 4.2). According to my market-edge hypothesis, the correlation should have been negative, not positive. Something was wrong.

If we look at the results for SKEW thresholds of less than or equal to 110 and 112.5 (Figure 4.2), the problem becomes obvious: entering iron condor trades when the SKEW index was very low was historically unprofitable. Not less profitable, but *unprofitable*. On average, these trades lost money.

Figure 4.2: 1TPS - IV SKEW Filter (RUT, SPX, NDX)					
SKEW-L Condition	SKEW Period	Profit Factor	% Winning Trades	Avg. Return on Margin	% of Total Trades
N/A (ALL)	N/A (ALL)	2.10	85.10%	3.22%	100.00%
SKEW ≤ 110.0	NA	0.63	61.15%	-3.41%	0.90%
SKEW ≤ 112.5	NA	0.91	71.48%	-0.68%	5.61%
SKEW ≤ 115.0	NA	1.28	77.46%	1.48%	12.62%
SKEW ≤ 117.5	NA	1.96	84.29%	3.32%	26.43%
SKEW ≤ 120.0	NA	2.31	86.21%	3.78%	45.75%
SKEW ≤ 122.5	NA	2.22	85.90%	3.58%	63.31%
SKEW ≤ 125.0	NA	2.24	85.99%	3.55%	76.43%
SKEW ≤ 127.5	NA	2.24	86.05%	3.51%	85.53%
SKEW ≤ 130.0	NA	2.27	86.24%	3.52%	91.34%
SKEW ≤ 132.5	NA	2.23	85.95%	3.44%	94.37%
SKEW ≤ 135.0	NA	2.18	85.65%	3.36%	96.46%
SKEW ≤ 137.5	NA	2.16	85.52%	3.32%	98.35%
Corr SKEW ≤ N	NA	NA	0.736	0.701	NA

To gain further insight into this surprising behavior, I split the SKEW filter table into two parts in Figure 4.3. The average SKEW index value over this period was approximately 120, so I used that value as a dividing line. For SKEW index values below 120, I examined trades that were entered when the SKEW index was *less than* or equal to the specified threshold. For SKEW index values above 120, I examined trades that were entered when the SKEW index was *greater than* or equal to the specified threshold. In other words, I examined what happened when iron condor trades were entered when the SKEW index approached the upper and lower tails of distribution.

Let's focus on the upper region first. As SKEW values increased, the profit factor, percentage of winning trades, and the average return on margin all declined. In addition, SKEW values above 132.5 actually led to negative iron condor returns.

The correlations between the SKEW filter threshold and the percentage of winning trades (-0.955) and average return on margin (-0.963) both approached negative one (Figure 4.3). In other words, the relationship was almost perfectly negatively correlated with the SKEW index threshold values, which is exactly what I hypothesized.

However, the performance relationship was exactly the *opposite* for SKEW index values below 120. The correlations between the SKEW threshold and the percentage of winning trades (+0.976) and average return on margin (+0.975) both approached *positive* one (Figure 4.3). In other words, the relationship was almost perfectly *positively* correlated with the SKEW index threshold values, which is exactly the *opposite* of what I initially hypothesized.

Figure 4.3: 1TPS - IV SKEW Filter (RUT, SPX, NDX)					
SKEW-L Condition	SKEW Period	Profit Factor	% Winning Trades	Avg. Return on Margin	% of Total Trades
N/A (ALL)	N/A (ALL)	2.10	85.10%	3.22%	100.00%
SKEW ≤ 110.0	NA	0.63	61.15%	-3.41%	0.90%
SKEW ≤ 112.5	NA	0.91	71.48%	-0.68%	5.61%
SKEW ≤ 115.0	NA	1.28	77.46%	1.48%	12.62%
SKEW ≤ 117.5	NA	1.96	84.29%	3.32%	26.43%
SKEW ≤ 120.0	NA	2.31	86.21%	3.78%	45.75%
Corr SKEW ≤ N	NA	NA	0.976	0.975	NA
SKEW ≥ 120.0	NA	1.93	84.19%	2.75%	54.29%
SKEW ≥ 122.5	NA	1.88	83.72%	2.60%	36.72%
SKEW ≥ 125.0	NA	1.69	82.24%	2.16%	23.57%
SKEW ≥ 127.5	NA	1.42	79.53%	1.51%	14.47%
SKEW ≥ 130.0	NA	1.01	73.15%	0.03%	8.66%
SKEW ≥ 132.5	NA	0.89	70.89%	-0.54%	5.63%
SKEW ≥ 135.0	NA	0.90	70.65%	-0.51%	3.58%
SKEW ≥ 137.5	NA	0.58	60.24%	-2.78%	1.65%
Corr SKEW ≥ N	NA	NA	-0.955	-0.963	NA
115 ≥ SKEW ≤ 120	NA	3.32	89.55%	4.66%	33.17%

Exercises like this are always educational, even for traders with over 30 years of experience. My proposed market-edge hypothesis accurately explains the inverse performance relationship for SKEW index values above 120, so how can we rationalize the direct or positive performance relationship below 120?

One possible explanation is that low SKEW index values systematically and consistently under-compensate options sellers for tail risk. However, this would imply that option traders represent the "dumb-money" when SKEW index values are low and the "smart-money" when SKEW index values are high. While that is certainly possible, it would be unusual.

If the asymmetric performance results in Figures 4.3 reflect a permanent and tradable market anomaly, it would imply that there is an exploitable sweet-spot in the center of the SKEW index. To confirm this, I calculated all three performance metrics for SKEW index values between 115 and 120 (Figure 4.3). The resulting profit factor was 3.32, the percentage of winning trades was 89.55%, and the average return on margin was 4.66%. All three metrics represent significant improvements relative to the unfiltered trade metrics: 2.10, 85.10%, and 3.22%.

There is no question that the filtered performance relationships are highly significant both above and below 120, but the results were not entirely consistent with my market-edge hypothesis. Given this inconsistency, I would not personally use the 115-120 SKEW index filter, despite its superior performance metrics.

That said, the SKEW performance results are intriguing and warrant further study. If these results are fully consistent with your market-edge hypothesis, the validation of your assumptions should give you additional confidence in using the SKEW index as a discriminating entry filter for the iron condor strategy and for related Delta-neutral option income strategies.

IV Percentile Rank Filter

The next discriminating filter example will be based on the implied volatility (IV) percentile rank. A percentile rank equals the percentage of distribution values that are less than or equal to a given data value. In this example, we are interested in the percentile rank of implied volatility (IV), which will be derived from the appropriate volatility index (SPX:VIX, RUT:RVX, NDX:VXN). Given the limited scope of this article, we will use a single period of 63 trading days (approximately three months) to calculate the percentile rank, but this exercise could be repeated with a number of shorter and longer periods.

If only 5% of the historical VIX values over the previous 63 trading days were less than or equal to the current VIX value, the current IV percentile rank would be 5%. In other words, the current level of implied volatility would near the *bottom* of the IV distribution from the preceding 63 trading days.

Similarly, if 90% of the historical VIX values over the previous 63 trading days were less than or equal to the current VIX value, the current IV percentile rank would be 90%. In this scenario, the current level of implied volatility would near the *top* of the IV distribution from the preceding 63 trading days.

Given your experience with iron condors and your understanding of implied volatility, try to develop your own market-edge hypothesis. What type of IV environment should generate the best risk-adjusted returns for the iron condor? What should happen at the extremes? Why?

* * *

Conventional wisdom suggests that iron condor trades should be entered when IV is "high." Why? Because, implied volatilities revert to the mean – eventually. Iron condors, like most option income strategies, have negative Vega, which means that the value of an iron condor increases when IV decreases and falls when IV rises. If we enter iron condor trades when the IV percentile rank is high and implied volatility is mean-reverting, then IV should decline, which would help our iron condor.

Does this sound reasonable? Depending on the period, I would have to say yes. Entering iron condors when the IV percentile rank is high should improve performance to some degree.

What about when the IV percentile rank is low? Conventional wisdom would suggest the iron condor would perform poorly in this environment. I would have to disagree. While volatility is mean reverting, the reversion process is much faster in a declining price and increasing volatility environment. Periods of gradually rising prices and falling IVs can continue for very long periods, well beyond 63 days. As a result, I would expect the performance metrics for iron condor trades to improve when IV percentile rank is low.

This raises a very important point: rising markets are very different from falling markets. We cannot assume that they are simply mirror images of each other. This is not the case. Very different strategies, variables, time periods, parameters, filters, etc. will be required to understand and trade up and down markets.

Understanding this, it becomes reasonable to hypothesize that both high and low IV percentile ranks could enhance iron condor performance. For that reason, I split the performance results for the IV percentile rank (Figure 4.4) into two sections, just as I did for the SKEW index. If my joint hypothesis is correct, we should see performance improve as the IV percentile rank thresholds increase or decrease from 50. In other words, the correlation between IV percentile rank threshold values and performance should be negative below 50 and positive above 50.

The best iron condor performance was generated when the IV percentile rank was less than or equal to 5%. The resulting profit factor of 2.91 exceeded the profit factor for all unfiltered trades (2.10). The percentage of winning trades increased from 85.10% to 88.05%, and the average return on margin increased from 3.22% to 4.18% (Figure 4.4). These were the best trade results we have examined so far.

In this region, the correlations between the IV percentile rank threshold and the percentage of winning trades (-0.986) and average return on margin (-0.986) both approached *negative* one. In other words, the relationship was almost perfectly *negatively* correlated with the IV percentile rank threshold values, which is consistent with my hypothesis, but contradicts conventional wisdom.

For IV percentile rank thresholds above 50, the best performing threshold value was 90%. The resulting profit factor of 2.38 exceeded the profit factor for all unfiltered trades (2.10). The percentage of winning trades increased from 85.10% to 87.61%, and the average return on margin increased from 3.22% to 3.75% (Figure 4.4).

In this region, the correlations between the IV percentile rank threshold and the percentage of winning trades (+0.986) and average return on margin (+0.962) both approached *positive* one. In other words, the relationship was almost perfectly *positively* correlated with the IV percentile rank. These results confirmed our market-edge hypothesis *and* validated conventional wisdom for high IV percentile ranks.

Figure 4.4: 1TPS - IV Rank(63) Filter (RUT, SPX, NDX)					
IV Rank Condition	IV Rank Period	Profit Factor	% Winning Trades	Avg. Return on Margin	% of Total Trades
N/A (ALL)	N/A (ALL)	2.10	85.10%	3.22%	100.00%
IV Rank ≤ 5.0	63	2.91	88.05%	4.18%	15.19%
IV Rank ≤ 10.0	63	2.78	87.63%	4.05%	21.36%
IV Rank ≤ 15.0	63	2.57	86.86%	3.82%	26.44%
IV Rank ≤ 20.0	63	2.52	86.64%	3.75%	31.48%
IV Rank ≤ 25.0	63	2.43	86.29%	3.64%	35.82%
IV Rank ≤ 30.0	63	2.35	86.02%	3.54%	39.90%
IV Rank ≤ 40.0	63	2.23	85.39%	3.37%	47.71%
IV Rank ≤ 50.0	63	2.12	84.88%	3.21%	55.62%
Corr IV Rank ≤ N	63	NA	-0.986	-0.986	NA
IV Rank ≥ 50.0	63	2.07	85.35%	3.23%	45.39%
IV Rank ≥ 60.0	63	2.11	85.75%	3.31%	37.05%
IV Rank ≥ 70.0	63	2.16	86.12%	3.39%	30.24%
IV Rank ≥ 75.0	63	2.19	86.42%	3.45%	26.67%
IV Rank ≥ 80.0	63	2.26	86.80%	3.54%	22.88%
IV Rank ≥ 85.0	63	2.29	87.14%	3.61%	19.05%
IV Rank ≥ 90.0	63	2.38	87.61%	3.75%	14.38%
IV Rank ≥ 95.0	63	2.28	87.58%	3.65%	9.65%
Corr IV Rank ≥ N	63	NA	0.986	0.962	NA

A well-reasoned market-edge hypothesis validated by the results of thousands of managed iron condor trades provides compelling evidence of an effective and practical discriminating trade entry filter.

RSI Filter

Our next discriminating filter will be based on one of the most popular and widely-used technical indicators: the relative strength index (RSI). The RSI was introduced by J. Welles Wilder in his 1978 book, *New Concepts in Technical Trading Systems.* You will recall that the directional movement indicator (DMI) we used in Chapter 2 was introduced in the same book.

The RSI is a momentum price oscillator with values ranging from zero to 100. I used a 21-day period to calculate the RSI filter performance metrics, which represents approximately one month of trading data. Similar RSI filter research could be replicated with shorter and longer periods.

To calculate the RSI index, we first calculate the intermediate relative strength (RS) value, which equals the average daily gains divided by the average daily losses over the specified lookback period. Several different types of moving averages can be used to calculate the intermediate relative strength (RS) term and I used a simple moving average. As a result, the average daily gain equals the sum of the daily gains divided by the number of days in the lookback period, 21 in this example. The same procedure is used to calculate the average daily loss. The intermediate relative strength (RS) value is then used to calculate the RSI, which is bounded by zero and 100.

RS = (Average Daily Gain / Average Daily Loss)

RSI = 100 – (100 / (1+RS))

RSI values above 50 represent positive momentum and RSI values below 50 represent negative momentum. In addition to its use as a momentum indicator, extreme values of RSI (75/25, 80/20, or 90/10) are often used as an indication of a pending reversal.

Before we review the results, I will again challenge you to develop your own market-edge hypothesis based on the 21-day RSI. What type of RSI values should generate the best risk-adjusted returns for the iron condor? Should the RSI be used as a momentum/trend indicator or as a reversal oscillator? What is likely to happen at the extreme values of the RSI? Should high RSI extremes be interpreted differently from low RSI extremes? Why?

* * *

Here are my thoughts on using the RSI as a discriminating filter. As I have explained several times, up markets are very different from down markets. Let's focus initially on recent periods of declining prices, or when RSI values are below 50. You will recall from the beginning of this chapter that I used a simple bullish pullback strategy to introduce discriminating filters. I speculated that pullbacks of increasing magnitude would generate improved bullish strategy performance – at least during long-term uptrends. As the magnitude of the pullback increased, the RSI would decrease. In other words, large pullbacks would correspond to very low RSI values.

If large pullbacks are followed by significant increases in the price of the underlying security, would this be good or bad for the iron condor? It would lead to significant losses. Remember that iron condors can lose money if prices decrease *or increase* by a greater amount than expected. In addition, due to the vertical skew, there is less protection to the upside. In other words, the strike price of the short call option is closer to the initial price of the underlying security than the strike price of the short put option. As a result, large bullish price moves would adversely affect performance.

So if large pullbacks are problematic for the iron condor, what about small pullbacks, RSI < 40 for example? What would happen to implied volatility if prices decline moderately? IV would increase. Since our iron condor is a net seller of options, the higher initial IV would provide some additional protection on both the upside and the downside. Since prices would have already declined by a moderate amount, it would reduce the likelihood of an incremental secondary move to the downside, but would not be overly bullish. This environment should be favorable for the iron condor and should generate excess returns. If this market-edge hypothesis is correct, we would expect to see a positive correlation between the RSI threshold and the performance metrics for RSI values below 50.

What about for RSI threshold values above 50? Let's revisit the iron condor results when the IV percentile rank values were very low (Figure 4.4). You will recall that the best performance metrics we have seen so far occurred when the IV percentile rank was less than or equal to 5%. Since IV and price are negatively correlated (Figure 4.1), price should be high when IV is low. If prices are high, that implies that RSI should be high as well. As a result, high values of RSI should correspond to improved iron condor performance. In this specific environment, RSI should be interpreted as a trend indicator, not as a reversal indicator. If this market-edge hypothesis is correct, we would expect to see a positive correlation between the RSI threshold and the performance metrics for RSI values above 50 as well.

Let's begin with a review of the performance results for RSI values below 50. The best iron condor performance in this region was generated when the RSI was less than or equal to 40% (Figure 4.5). The resulting profit factor of 2.81 exceeded the profit factor for all unfiltered trades (2.10). The percentage of winning trades increased from 85.10% to 88.70%, and the average return on margin increased from 3.22% to 4.36%. These results are very consistent with the best IV percentile rank results.

In this region, the correlations between the RSI threshold and the percentage of winning trades (+0.956) and average return on margin (+0.956) both approached *positive* one. In other words, the relationship was almost perfectly *positively* correlated with the RSI threshold values, which is consistent with our hypothesis.

For RSI thresholds above 50, the best performing threshold value was 90, which resulted in 100% winning trades (Figure 4.5). Before we get too excited, I should point out it was very rare for 21-day RSI values to exceed 90 (only 0.04% of all unfiltered trades). However, if we look at RSI values greater than or equal to 80, the results were still impressive. The resulting profit factor of 3.13 significantly exceeded the profit factor for all unfiltered trades (2.10). The percentage of winning trades increased from 85.10% to 88.10%, and the average return on margin increased from 3.22% to 3.92%.

For RSI values above 50, the correlations between the RSI threshold and the percentage of winning trades (+0.886) and average return on margin (+0.897) were not quite as high as the IV percentile rank correlation, but were still very high. The RSI filtered results confirmed our market-edge hypothesis over the entire RSI spectrum.

Figure 4.5: 1TPS -RSI(21) Filter (RUT, SPX, NDX)					
RSI Condition	RSI Period	Profit Factor	% Winning Trades	Avg. Return on Margin	% of Total Trades
N/A (ALL)	N/A (ALL)	2.10	85.10%	3.22%	100.00%
RSI ≤ 10.0	21	2.12	84.94%	3.00%	3.96%
RSI ≤ 20.0	21	2.17	85.16%	3.08%	4.02%
RSI ≤ 30.0	21	2.70	87.71%	4.00%	6.06%
RSI ≤ 40.0	21	2.81	88.70%	4.36%	18.98%
Corr RSI ≤ N	21	NA	0.956	0.956	NA
RSI ≥ 60.0	21	2.05	84.68%	2.94%	31.73%
RSI ≥ 70.0	21	2.49	87.39%	3.43%	9.97%
RSI ≥ 80.0	21	3.13	88.10%	3.92%	2.02%
RSI ≥ 90.0	21	infinite	100.00%	6.91%	0.04%
Corr RSI ≥ N	21	NA	0.886	0.897	NA

As was the case with the IV percentile rank, a well-reasoned market-edge hypothesis validated by the results of thousands of managed iron condor trades provides compelling evidence of an effective and practical discriminating RSI trade entry filter.

Term Structure of Volatilities Filter

The final discriminating filter we will analyze in this chapter is based on the term structure of volatilities, which is a function of the *horizontal* IV skew. In this article, we have focused on the vertical skew, which captures the relationship between implied volatility and strike prices. The horizontal skew represents the relationship between implied volatility and time to expiration. As a result, the horizontal skew and the term structure of volatilities can be used to estimate the expected level of implied volatility in the future.

In this article, we are using each underlying security's volatility index as a proxy for implied volatility. The best-known volatility index is the CBOE Volatility index or VIX, which provides a single objective measure of the expected 30-day volatility, derived from the prices of S&P 500 (SPX) equity index options.

The VIX index itself is not a tradable instrument, but there is an active and highly liquid futures market based on the VIX index. There are weekly and monthly VIX futures contracts that are cash-settled based on the value of the VIX index at futures expiration. It is possible to use the prices of all VIX futures contracts to construct a precise, real-time term structure of volatilities. The prices of the VIX futures contracts provide a tradable estimate of the market's expected level of volatility at any point in the future.

To create a discriminating filter based on the term structure of volatilities (TSVol), I calculated the spread between the VIX index and the interpolated 30-day forward VIX price. I used the prices of the first two monthly VIX futures contracts to interpolate an estimate of the 30-day forward VIX index.

A brief example should help illustrate the process. Let's assume the value of the VIX index was 12.50 and the prices of the first two monthly VIX futures contracts were 15.00 and 16.00. Furthermore, let's assume the first two contracts had 15 and 45 days remaining until expiration. The resulting estimate of the 30-day forward VIX index would be 15.50 (0.50 * 15.00 + 0.50 * 16.00). In this example, the resulting VIX zero to 30-day spread would equal 3.00 (15.50 − 12.50), which implies the VIX index would be expected to increase by 3.00% (from 12.50 to 15.50) in the next 30 calendar days.

The weights of the two monthly futures contracts are designed to maintain a constant 30-day forward estimate of the VIX index (0.50 * 15 days + 0.50 * 45 days = 30 days). As time passes, the weight of the front-month contract declines and the weight of the back-month contact increases. The sum of the two weights always equals 1.0 or 100%.

Let's take the above example a step further and try to cultivate the insight required to design and test a market-edge hypothesis based on the term structure of volatilities. In the above example, the VIX index was 12.50 and the zero to 30-day VIX spread was 3.00, which implies an expected VIX index of 15.50 in 30 days.

A VIX index value of 12.50 is quite low. The average VIX index from 2000 through September 2016 was 20.44. This average is a little misleading due to some very high values during recessionary periods, but the median VIX index value of 18.51 was still much higher than 12.50. In fact, a VIX index value of 12.50 corresponded to a percentile rank of approximately 10% during this period. In other words, the example VIX index value of 12.50 was only higher than roughly 10% of the historical end-of-day VIX index observations from 2000 through September 2016.

We have already examined the iron condor results when implied volatility was low. Specifically, we saw that when the 63-day IV percentile rank was less than or equal to 5%, the performance metrics for the iron condor dominated the unfiltered trade results (Figure 4.4).

We also know that implied volatility of SPX options (the VIX) and the price of SPX are negatively correlated (Figure 4.1). In other words, when IV was low, SPX prices were high. We tested the iron condor results when prices were high; we observed that when the 21-day RSI was above 80, the iron condor results were significantly better than the unfiltered results across all performance metrics (Figure 4.5). When the RSI was above 90, there were no losing iron condor trades. As a result, we would expect the specific VIX term structure example described above to be a very favorable environment for the iron condor.

However, I have still not explained *why* the VIX 0-30 spread (+3.00) was so wide in the preceding example. Why would the term structure of volatilities be so steep when the VIX index was unusually low? Why would market participants expect the VIX index to increase by 3% in the subsequent 30 calendar days? The answer is the driving force behind the price structure of the term structure of volatilities.

* * *

The answer is mean reversion. As I have already explained, volatility is generally assumed to be mean-reverting. And it always is – eventually. The long-term correlation between the VIX 0-30 day spread and the VIX index is -0.569 (not shown). Low VIX values are associated with large spreads and high VIX values are associated with low or even negative VIX 0-30 day spreads. The lower the VIX, the faster the market expects it to increase and vice versa.

This is a market anomaly. In fact, it represents one of the most significant and exploitable market anomalies and it affects several different markets: options, volatility futures, and volatility ETFs. *The market consistently overestimates the speed of volatility mean-reversion, specifically when prices are high and IV is low.*

We have already seen indirect evidence of this. We observed that the iron condor performed very well in low IV (Figure 4.4) and high RSI (Figure 4.5) environments. We concluded that periods of high prices and low volatilities tend to persist and are not immediately followed by sharp reversals. In fact, an external shock is often required to jolt the market out of complacency. Therefore, our market-edge hypothesis would conclude that high VIX 0-30 day spreads should generate excess risk-adjusted iron condor returns. We would expect to see a positive correlation between the VIX 0-30 spread threshold values and the performance metrics.

Were we correct? Absolutely. The volatility term structure results were very consistent with the low IV (Figure 4.4) and high RSI (Figure 4.5) environments. The best performing filter threshold was for VIX 0-30 spreads above 4.0 (Figure 4.6). The resulting profit factor of 4.26 more than doubled the profit factor for all unfiltered trades (2.10). The percentage of winning trades increased from 85.10% to 91.08%, and the average return on margin increased from 3.22% to 3.78%. These results are consistent with the best IV percentile rank and RSI performance metrics. In fact, the profit factor of 4.26 is the best we have seen so far.

The correlations between the VIX 0-30 spread threshold and the percentage of winning trades (+0.485) and average return on margin (+0.574) were both positive (Figure 4.6), but were not as high as the correlations of previous filter thresholds we have examined. In this case, the relationship between the VIX 0-30 spread and the performance metrics was positive, but was not linear. The VIX 0-30 spread had very little impact when the spread was low, but was highly significant when the spread was high. This non-linearity would not compromise the efficacy of the VIX 0-30 spread discriminating filter in practice.

Figure 4.6: 1TPS -TSVol Filter (RUT, SPX, NDX)				
Minimum VIX 0 - 30 Spread	Profit Factor	% Winning Trades	Avg. Return on Margin	% of Total Trades
N/A (ALL)	2.10	85.10%	3.22%	100.00%
≥ -10.0	2.12	85.19%	3.23%	98.89%
≥ -5.0	2.20	85.53%	3.34%	97.80%
≥ 0.0	2.09	81.99%	3.12%	81.99%
≥ 1.0	2.00	84.35%	2.94%	57.66%
≥ 2.0	2.55	87.20%	3.71%	27.13%
≥ 3.0	3.94	91.08%	4.79%	10.54%
≥ 4.0	4.26	91.08%	4.93%	3.78%
Corr VIX 0 - 30 Spread	NA	0.485	0.574	NA

This chapter introduced discriminating filters and demonstrated the thought-process required to design and test market-edge hypotheses. The results for many different filter thresholds were provided, several of which were consistent with the market-edge hypothesis. All of these discriminating filters could easily be replicated and applied in real-time. The next chapter will take discriminating filters to the next level.

5 - OIS UNIVERSAL FILTER

The unfiltered performance metrics described in Chapter 2 demonstrate that managed iron condor trades have been profitable historically, even when entered indiscriminately, with no attempt to identify or capitalize on optimal entry conditions. In fact, many traders use a similar unfiltered monthly or weekly campaign approach, dutifully entering new option income positions every month or every week, irrespective of the market environment.

There is nothing inherently wrong with this approach; properly managed, monthly option income campaigns should deliver excess returns. However, the superior performance metrics in Chapter 4 reveal that it is possible to use market-edge hypotheses and discriminating filters to systematically identify superior trading environments.

Despite this success, I wanted a new metric that was even more robust than a discriminating filter based on a single technical or fundamental indicator. I have been trading and studying option income strategies for many years and I have spent many years developing, analyzing, and testing many different types of filters. The Option Income Strategy (OIS) Universal Filter represents the culmination of my research efforts.

The OIS Universal Filter (OISUF) is a standardized metric calculated by an algorithm that exclusively uses historical and current prices and implied volatilities. The volatility index is used as a proxy for implied volatility, which limits the application of the OISUF to underlying securities that have corresponding volatility indices.

The OISUF algorithm has very few parameters. It captures the fundamental relationships between price, implied volatility, and OIS performance. It was not derived from a specific dataset and the *parameters were not optimized.* As a result, the *parameters in the algorithm will never change and will never be re-estimated.* The limited number of non-optimized parameters greatly enhances the robustness of the OISUF.

Optimizing a large number of parameters to maximize in-sample strategy performance is essentially data-mining, which greatly magnifies the risk of identifying spurious correlations instead of meaningful exploitable relationships - relationships that will persist in the future. If we examine enough parameter combinations, we will *always* find a few that generated excess returns *in the historical dataset*.

Unfortunately, most of these optimized strategies that rely on over-fitted parameter combinations fail miserably in subsequent periods. This is why I have repeatedly stressed the importance of developing a well-reasoned market-edge hypothesis first, then testing the historical results against the hypothesis, and only allocating capital to strategies that generate results that are consistent with the initial hypothesis.

Unlike strategies that employ data-mining techniques to optimize a large number of parameter values, the OISUF algorithm was derived directly from the market-edge hypothesis. The OISUF uses very few parameters and the parameter values were not optimized. Instead, the parameter values were structural and were chosen before strategy testing. Structural means the OISUF parameter values were a byproduct of the market-edge hypothesis itself. They were the only parameter values tested. Despite the use of structural, pre-determined parameter values, the OISUF algorithm is very responsive to changing market conditions. It can be used to systematically quantify the attractiveness of OIS trade entry environments in real time.

I call it the OIS Universal Filter because it can be applied to enhance the risk-adjusted returns of option income strategies almost universally. It is applicable to any Delta-neutral option income strategy that does not require time (calendar) spread components. This includes the butterfly, iron-butterfly, condor, iron condor, road trip, weirdor, kevlar, jeep, and many other exotic hybrid strategies. Despite the wide range of OISUF applicable strategies, they will all have negative Gamma, positive Theta, and negative Vega by definition.

As an aside, time and diagonal spreads require selling near-term options and purchasing longer-term options to generate positive Theta. As a result, the performance of time-spread strategies is heavily dependent on the term structure of volatilities. As a result, time spreads are actually directional volatility strategies, which require a *unique* type of trade entry filter. These time-spread-specific filters are fascinating, but are beyond the scope of this article.

The OIS Universal Filter will yield the best results when applied to option income strategies that respond gradually to changes in the price of the underlying security (those with relatively flat T+0 lines) and are profitable over a wide range of underlying security prices at option expiration. As already mentioned, the strategies should also employ minimal adjustments.

OISUF Performance Metrics

The OIS Universal Filter algorithm produces a standardized OIS score. In this context, the word "standardized" means the resulting OIS scores are directly comparable across all underlying securities. OIS scores are not bounded, but typically fall between negative 200 and positive 100.

Scores below zero indicate unfavorable OIS environments and scores above zero signify favorable OIS environments. Furthermore, higher OIS scores imply more advantageous OIS environments across the entire spectrum of prospective OIS values. For example, an OIS score of 100 should generate better risk-adjusted returns than a score of 60, than a score of 20, than a score of negative 20, than a score of negative 60. The greater the deviation of the OIS scores from zero (positive or negative), the more significant the expected performance difference from the unfiltered trade data.

I will explain further about the OISUF later in this chapter, but let's now review the OISUF performance metrics in Figure 5.1. As has been the case throughout this article, the term "1TPS" in the table title means one trade per signal, which generated a new managed iron condor trade every day on the RUT, SPX, and NDX, provided the specific filter conditions were met.

The first two columns on the left-side of Figure 5.1 describe the OISUF condition. For OIS score threshold values of less than zero, the filter condition required OIS scores to be less than or equal to the threshold value. For OIS score threshold values of greater than or equal to zero, the filter condition required OIS scores to be greater than or equal to the threshold value. As the OIS score threshold deviated further from zero, the conditions became increasingly restrictive.

The next three columns show the performance metrics (profit factor, percentage of winning trades, and average return on margin) for each filter condition. The final column documents the percentage of the 15,434 managed iron condor trades that met the OISUF conditions.

To facilitate comparison with the filtered results, the first row in Figure 5.1 restates the performance metrics for all 15,434 unfiltered iron condor trades. As you will recall, the unfiltered managed iron condor strategy performed well historically. The unfiltered profit factor was 2.10 (2.10 dollars of gains per dollar of losses). In addition, 85.10% of the unfiltered trades were profitable and the average return on margin was 3.22%.

Beginning at the top of the table, OIS score thresholds of less than or equal to negative 120 produced unprofitable trades. In other words, the profit factors were all less than 1.0 and the average returns on margin were all negative. This is what we would expect for the worst (most negative) OIS scores and is consistent with the market-edge hypothesis.

OIS score thresholds of negative 100 to negative 20 produced profitable iron condor trades and profitability increased as the OIS score increased. We would expect to see increasing profitability as a function of rising OIS scores. However, should the iron condor strategy be profitable in this region of negative OIS scores? Why would that be the case?

* * *

The iron condor strategy was still profitable in this region because of the inherent profitability of option income strategies, particularly when these strategies are employed using chronically overvalued options on the equity indices. Instead of comparing the results to a break-even baseline, the results should be compared to the unfiltered performance metrics. In other words, how did the results for OIS score thresholds of negative 100 to negative 20 compare to the unfiltered trade results?

As we would expect, the negative OIS thresholds produced worse results than the unfiltered trades. For every filter condition in this region, the profit factor, percentage of winning trades, and return on margin were worse (lower) than the unfiltered performance metrics.

The opposite was true for all OIS score thresholds above zero. In every such case, the profit factor, percentage of winning trades, and average return on margin exceeded the unfiltered performance metrics. The metrics improved as the OIS score threshold increased. The performance metrics for OIS scores of 40, 60, 80, and 100 were exceptional: profit factors from 5.15 to 20.69, 92.89% to 98.36% winning trades, and average returns of 5.53% to 8.13%.

As was the case for negative OIS scores, all three performance metrics were an increasing function of the OIS scores for positive OIS thresholds. In fact, there was only a single case when the performance metrics did not increase for a corresponding increase in OIS score. This occurred for an OIS score threshold of 80. This is likely the result of the small number of trades in this region.

Despite this minor inconsistency, the correlation between the OIS score threshold and the percentage of winning trades was 0.996. The correlation between the OIS score threshold and the average return on margin was 0.994. Both performance metrics were almost perfectly positively correlated with the OIS score threshold.

Figure 5.1: 1TPS - OIS Filter (RUT, SPX, NDX)					
OIS Condition	OIS Score Threshold	Profit Factor	% Winning Trades	Avg. Return on Margin	% of Total Trades
N/A (ALL)	N/A (ALL)	2.10	85.10%	3.22%	100.00%
OIS Score <=	-200	0.63	61.72%	-3.67%	0.83%
OIS Score <=	-180	0.70	64.25%	-2.87%	1.25%
OIS Score <=	-160	0.77	66.53%	-1.99%	1.53%
OIS Score <=	-140	0.84	68.66%	-1.34%	1.84%
OIS Score <=	-120	0.89	70.18%	-0.83%	2.22%
OIS Score <=	-100	1.16	75.32%	0.99%	3.07%
OIS Score <=	-80	1.25	77.01%	1.40%	4.20%
OIS Score <=	-60	1.47	80.30%	2.19%	6.97%
OIS Score <=	-40	1.65	82.58%	2.57%	13.54%
OIS Score <=	-20	1.98	84.89%	3.16%	27.18%
OIS Score >=	0	2.29	85.86%	3.46%	49.59%
OIS Score >=	20	2.80	87.78%	4.10%	25.14%
OIS Score >=	40	5.15	92.89%	5.53%	11.12%
OIS Score >=	60	7.52	95.32%	6.34%	4.15%
OIS Score >=	80	6.01	94.27%	6.45%	1.24%
OIS Score >=	100	20.69	98.36%	8.13%	0.40%
OIS Score Correlation		N/A	0.996	0.994	N/A

There is a lot of data in Figure 5.1 and it can be challenging to grasp all of the data relationships from tabular data. As a result, I also created four charts that illustrate the same data graphically.

Figure 5.2 shows the relationship between profit factor and the OIS score threshold. As you will recall, a profit factor of 1.0 represents break-even. The profit factor formula is not a linear function of profitability, which is why the profit factor increases sharply at high OIS values.

Figure 5.3 demonstrates the relationship between the percentage of winning trades and the OIS score threshold. As you can see from the graph, the relationship is almost linear, which is consistent with the very high OIS score correlation of 0.996.

Figure 5.4 illustrates the relationship between the average return on margin and the OIS score threshold. As was the case for the percentage of winning trades, the relationship is almost linear, which is consistent with the very high OIS score correlation of 0.994.

Finally, Figure 5.5 shows the percentage of total trades that met the OISUF criteria as a function of the OIS score threshold. The OIS median value was very close to zero. As the OIS score threshold deviated from zero, the conditions became increasingly restrictive, resulting in fewer passing trades.

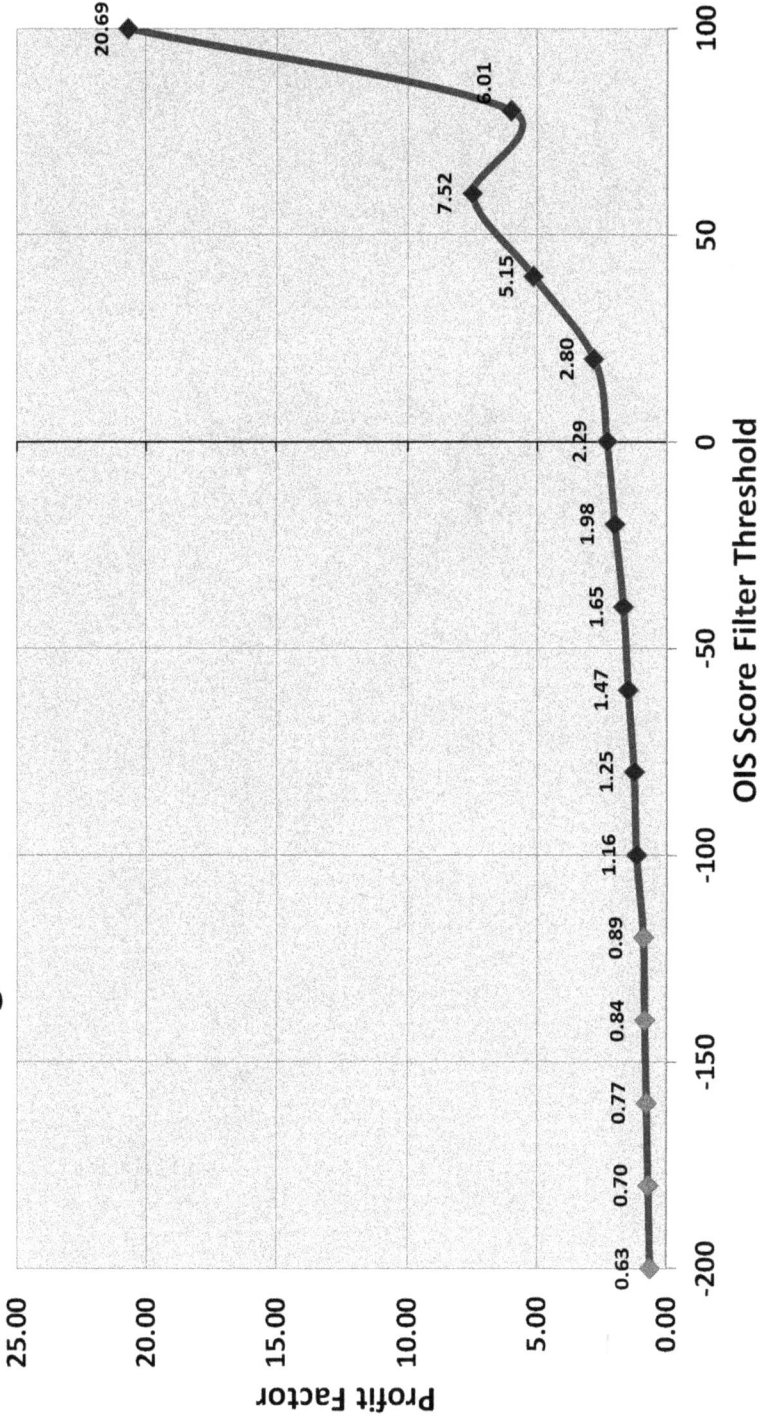

Figure 5.2: Profit Factor vs. OIS Score

Figure 5.3: % Winning Trades vs. OIS Score

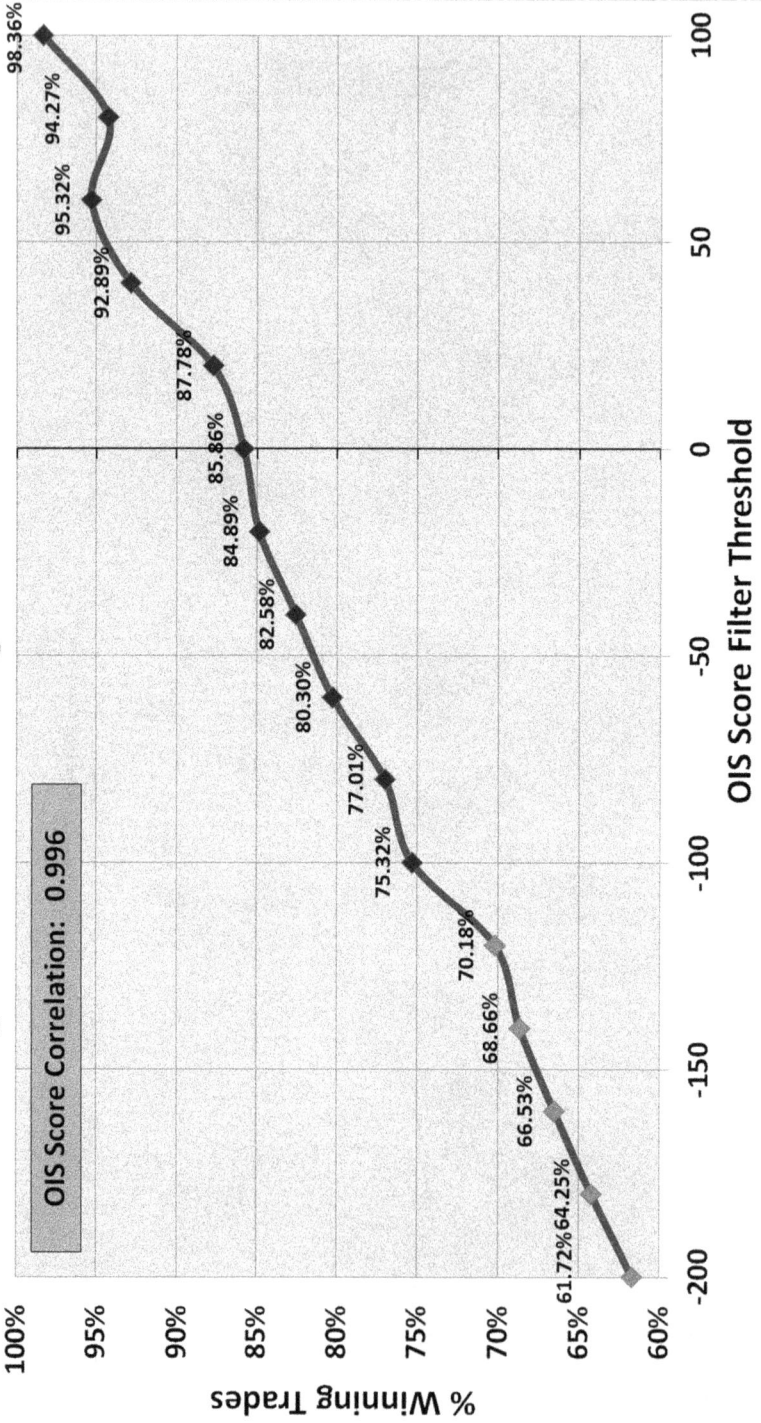

OIS Score Correlation: 0.996

98.36%
94.27%
95.32%
92.89%
87.78%
85.86%
84.89%
82.58%
80.30%
77.01%
75.32%
70.18%
68.66%
66.53%
61.72% 64.25%

% Winning Trades

OIS Score Filter Threshold

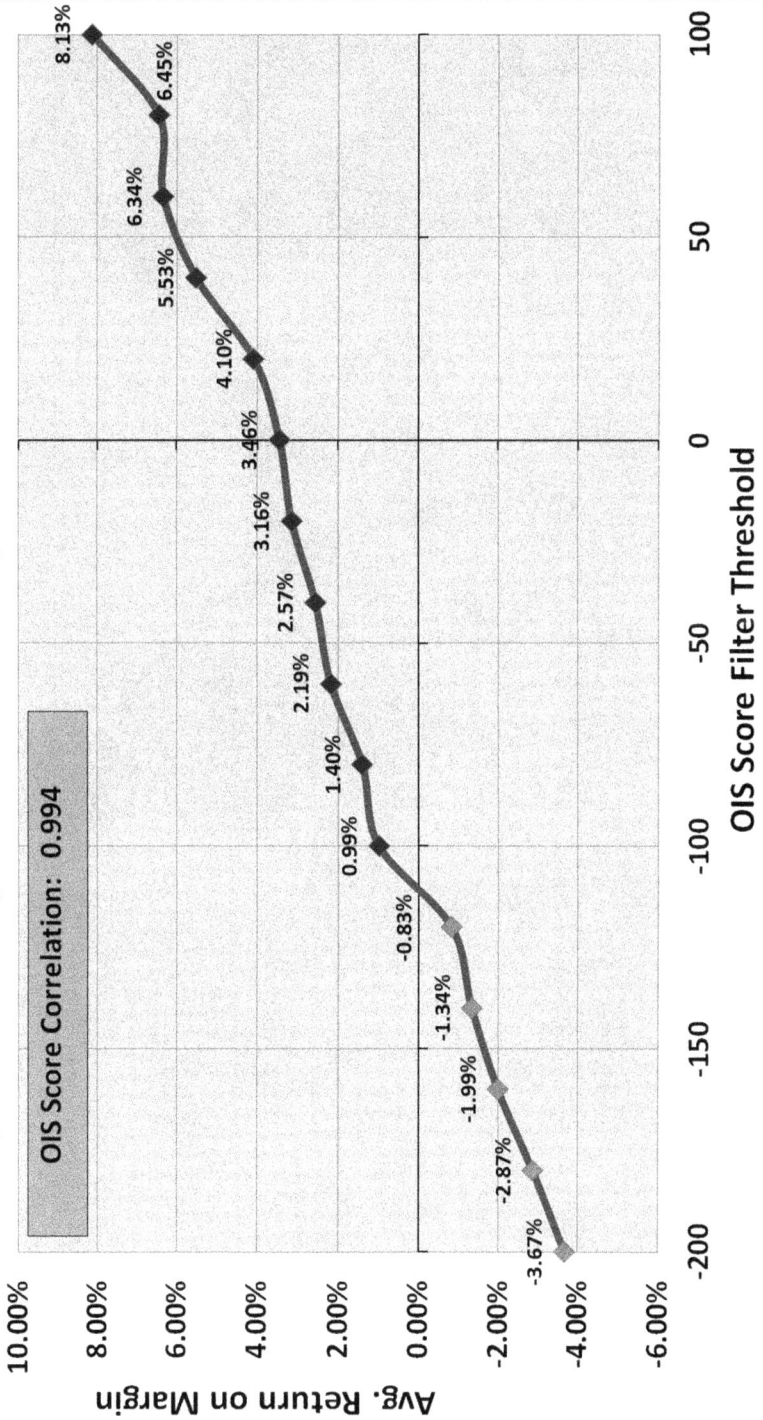

Figure 5.4: Avg. Return on Margin vs. OIS Score

OIS Score Correlation: 0.994

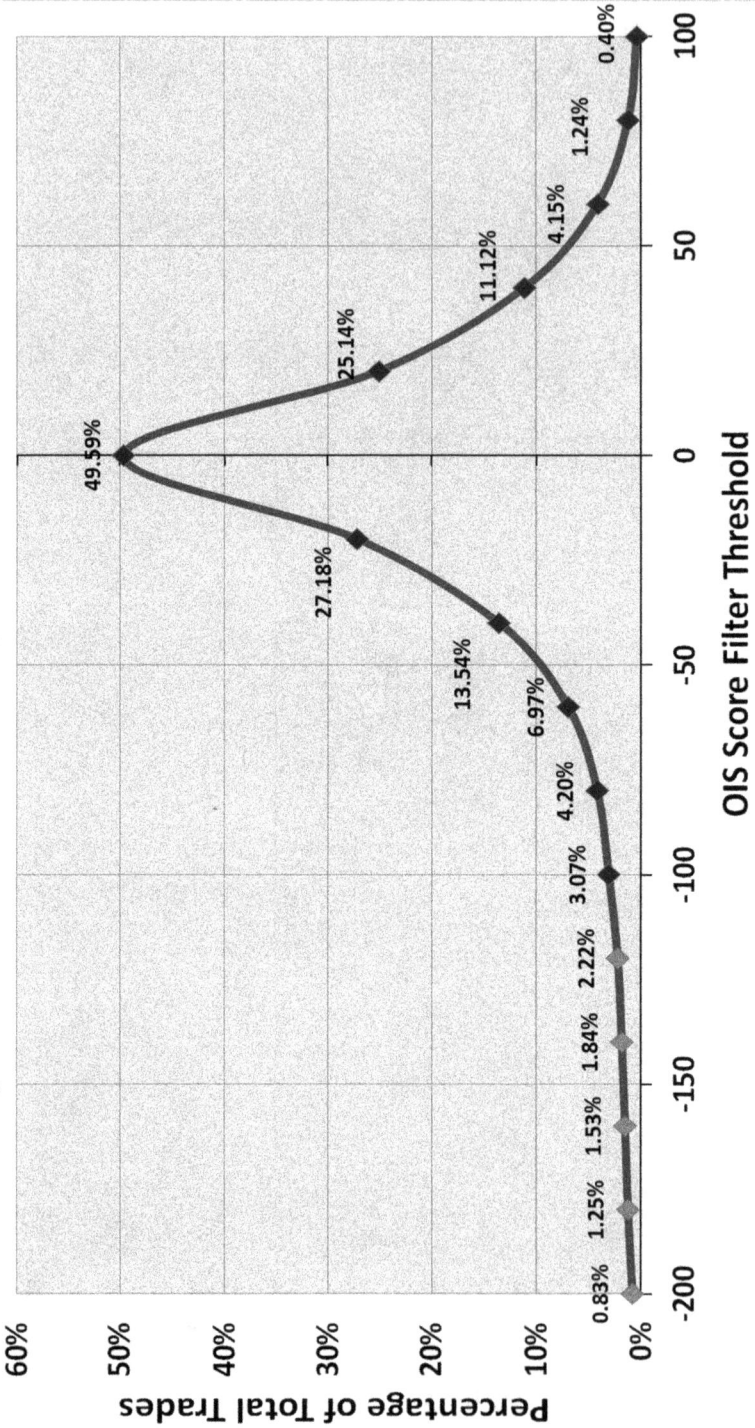

Figure 5.5: % of Total Trades vs. OIS Score

Combined Filters: OISUF & Price

One important advantage of the OIS Universal Filter is that its unique structural characteristics are independent from the other types of filters, including those we have examined in this article. That independence suggests we should be able to use the OISUF in conjunction with other filters to generate performance metrics that are superior to those generated by individual filters. The balance of this chapter will document the results from combining the OISUF with the filters presented in previous chapters.

The joint filter results will share a consistent tabular format. To facilitate comparison with the unfiltered results, the first data row in each of the following performance exhibits will restate the performance metrics for all 15,434 unfiltered iron condor trades. The second row will repeat the results for the OIS filter condition with OIS scores greater than or equal to 40. I could have selected a different OIS filter threshold example, but OIS scores above 40 generated excellent performance metrics without eliminating an excessive number of trades.

The next row of data will restate the performance metrics for the second (non-OISUF) filter, calculated independently (without the OISUF). In our first example (Figure 5.6), this condition includes trades when the price of the underlying security was greater than or equal to its 250-day moving average.

The bottom data row or rows of each table will show the performance metrics for combining the specific OISUF filter condition with the secondary filter conditions. The combined filters require that *all* specified filter conditions are met simultaneously. Ideally, the combined filter conditions will generate performance metrics that are superior to *both* the OISUF condition metrics and the secondary filter condition metrics.

In the first example (Figure 5.6) the OISUF 40+ filter condition was combined with a single moving average price condition (250-days) and multiple moving average price conditions (150-days & 250-days). As you will recall, despite a plausible market-edge hypothesis, the individual moving average price filters were largely ineffective in enhancing the iron condor performance results.

However, by adding the OISUF 40+ requirement to the moving average price filters, the resulting combined filters were able to generate higher profit factors and higher percentages of winning trades than either filter individually. However, it was somewhat disappointing that the combined average returns on margin were virtually unchanged from the individual OISUF filter results.

Figure 5.6: 1TPS - MA Price & OIS 40 (RUT, SPX, NDX)				
OIS Condition	OIS Score Threshold	Profit Factor	% Winning Trades	Avg. Return on Margin
N/A (ALL)	N/A (ALL)	2.10	85.10%	3.22%
OIS Score >=	40	5.15	92.89%	5.53%
Condition	Moving Average Period	Profit Factor	% Winning Trades	Avg. Return on Margin
Price >= MA	250	2.20	85.81%	3.19%
Price ≥ MA & OIS Score ≥ 40	250	6.39	94.27%	5.54%
Price ≥ MA1,MA2 & OIS Score ≥ 40	150, 250	6.72	94.43%	5.55%

Combined Filters: OISUF & Implied Volatility (IV)

Similar to the moving average price filters, the individual moving average IV filters were also mostly ineffective in enhancing the performance results. However, by adding the OISUF 40+ requirement to the 200-day moving average IV filter (Figure 5.7), the resulting combined filter generated significantly higher performance metrics: profit factor of 7.97, 94.50% winning trades, and an average return on margin of 5.80%.

Out of curiosity, I added the 250-day moving average price filter to the combined OISUF/IV filter and the results improved even further: profit factor of 8.46, 95.49% winning trades, and an average return on margin of 5.81%. It is encouraging that the OISUF 40+ filter was able to improve the results of individual filters that were unproductive individually.

Figure 5.7: 1TPS - MA IV & OIS 40 (RUT, SPX, NDX)

OIS Condition	OIS Score Threshold	Profit Factor	% Winning Trades	Avg. Return on Margin
N/A (ALL)	N/A (ALL)	2.10	85.10%	3.22%
OIS Score >=	40	5.15	92.89%	5.53%

Implied Volatility Index Condition	Moving Average Period	Profit Factor	% Winning Trades	Avg. Return on Margin
IV <= MA	200	2.20	85.48%	3.22%
IV ≤ MA & OIS Score ≥ 40	200	7.97	94.50%	5.80%
Price ≥ MA & IV ≤ MA & OIS Score ≥ 40	Price 250, IV 200	8.46	95.49%	5.81%

Combined Filters: OISUF & DMI

Similar to the moving average filters, DMI filters were also unsuccessful in materially enhancing the performance results. However, by adding the OISUF 40+ requirement to the 50-day DMI filter (Figure 5.8), the resulting combined filter generated significantly higher performance metrics than either individual filter: profit factor of 6.64, 93.45% winning trades, and an average return on margin of 5.56%. Once again, the OISUF 40+ filter was able to improve the results of filters that were ineffective individually.

Figure 5.8: 1TPS - DMI & OIS 40 (RUT, SPX, NDX)

OIS Condition	OIS Score Threshold	Profit Factor	% Winning Trades	Avg. Return on Margin
N/A (ALL)	N/A (ALL)	2.10	85.10%	3.22%
OIS Score >=	40	5.15	92.89%	5.53%

DMI Condition	DMI Period	Profit Factor	% Winning Trades	Avg. Return on Margin
DMI > 0	50	2.25	85.36%	3.26%
DMI > 0 & OIS Score ≥ 40	50	6.64	93.45%	5.56%

Combined Filters: OISUF & CBOE IV SKEW

I was able to find a narrow CBOE SKEW index range (115-120) that delivered superior performance metrics relative to the unfiltered trades. However, as you may recall from Chapter 4, the results were not entirely consistent with my market-edge hypothesis, which is why I rejected the use of the SKEW filter in my personal trading. That said, I was interested to see the combined filter results when adding the OISUF 40+ filter to the 115-120 SKEW filter condition.

Adding the OISUF 40+ requirement to the 115-120 SKEW filter did not increase the profit factor relative to the individual OISUF 40+ filter condition (Figure 5.9). However, the percentage of winning trades (93.04%) and average return on margin (5.81%) were slightly improved. The OISUF 40+ filter was able to enhance the results of the SKEW filter slightly, but only in two of the three metrics. I already questioned the use of the 115-120 SKEW filter in practice and the combined filter results reinforced my earlier conclusions.

Figure 5.9: 1TPS - CBOE IV SKEW & OIS 40 (RUT, SPX, NDX)				
OIS Condition	**OIS Score Threshold**	**Profit Factor**	**% Winning Trades**	**Avg. Return on Margin**
N/A (ALL)	N/A (ALL)	2.10	85.10%	3.22%
OIS Score >=	40	5.15	92.89%	5.53%
SKEW-L Condition	**SKEW Period**	**Profit Factor**	**% Winning Trades**	**Avg. Return on Margin**
115 ≤ SKEW ≤ 120	NA	3.32	89.55%	4.66%
115 ≤ SKEW ≤ 120 & OIS Score ≥ 40	NA	5.11	93.04%	5.81%

Combined Filters: OISUF & IV Percentile Rank

Unlike the trend filters in Chapter 3, the discriminating filters in Chapter 4 were generally able to improve upon the performance metrics of the unfiltered trades. The next secondary filter condition we will examine will be the 63-day IV percentile rank of less than or equal to 10%.

Adding the OISUF 40+ requirement to the IV percentile rank filter condition generated somewhat higher performance metrics than either individual filter: profit factor of 5.46, 93.55% winning trades, and an average return on margin of 5.53% (Figure 5.10).

Figure 5.10: 1TPS - IV Rank & OIS 40 (RUT, SPX, NDX)				
OIS Condition	OIS Score Threshold	Profit Factor	% Winning Trades	Avg. Return on Margin
N/A (ALL)	N/A (ALL)	2.10	85.10%	3.22%
OIS Score >=	40	5.15	92.89%	5.53%
IV Rank	IV Rank Period	Profit Factor	% Winning Trades	Avg. Return on Margin
IV Rank ≤ 10.0	63	2.78	87.63%	4.05%
IV Rank ≤ 10.0 & OIS Score ≥ 40	63	5.46	93.55%	5.53%

Combined Filters: OISUF & RSI

In Chapter 4, we also found that the 21-day discriminating RSI filter was useful in enhancing the iron condor strategy returns. Adding the OISUF 40+ requirement to the 21-day RSI filter generated *dramatically* higher performance metrics than either individual filter: profit factor of 26.38, 98.58% winning trades, and an average return on margin of 7.77% (Figure 5.11). The combined filter results were remarkable.

Figure 5.11: 1TPS - RSI(21) & OIS 40 (RUT, SPX, NDX)				
OIS Condition	OIS Score Threshold	Profit Factor	% Winning Trades	Avg. Return on Margin
N/A (ALL)	N/A (ALL)	2.10	85.10%	3.22%
OIS Score >=	40	5.15	92.89%	5.53%
RSI	RSI Period	Profit Factor	% Winning Trades	Avg. Return on Margin
RSI ≤ 40.0	21	2.81	88.70%	4.36%
RSI ≤ 40 & OIS Score ≥ 40	21	26.38	98.58%	7.77%

Combined Filters: OISUF & Term Structure of IV

In Chapter 4, we found that the term structure of volatilities was one of the best discriminating filters and was very useful in enhancing the iron condor strategy returns. Adding the OISUF 40+ requirement to the VIX 0-30 spread filter generated *significantly* higher performance metrics than either individual filter: profit factor of 25.26, 97.85% winning trades, and an average return on margin of 6.55% (Figure 5.12). The combined filter results were very impressive.

Figure 5.12: 1TPS - TSVol 4.0 & OIS 40 (RUT, SPX, NDX)				
OIS Condition	OIS Score Threshold	Profit Factor	% Winning Trades	Avg. Return on Margin
N/A (ALL)	N/A (ALL)	2.10	85.10%	3.22%
OIS Score >=	40	5.15	92.89%	5.53%
Minimum VIX 0 - 30 Spread	Period	Profit Factor	% Winning Trades	Avg. Return on Margin
> 4.0	NA	4.26	91.08%	4.93%
VIX 0 - 30 ≥ 4.0 & OIS Score ≥ 40	NA	25.26	97.85%	6.55%

OIS Universal Filter Conclusions

As I already explained, the OISUF algorithm has very few parameters. It captures the fundamental relationships between price, implied volatility, and OIS performance. It was not derived from a specific dataset and the *parameters were not optimized*. As a result, the *parameters in the algorithm will never change and will never be re-estimated.* The parameter values were structural and were chosen before strategy testing and they were the only parameter values tested. The limited number of non-optimized parameters greatly enhances the robustness of the OISUF.

The very high correlations between the OIS score threshold and performance metrics (Figure 5.1) and the outstanding performance of the OISUF as a stand-alone filter provide compelling evidence in support of its market-edge hypothesis and the corresponding OISUF algorithm.

Furthermore, the structural independence of the OISUF from other technical and fundamental filters makes it possible to combine the OISUF with other filters to deliver results that are superior to individual filters. Surprisingly, this was even possible for filters that were largely ineffective in enhancing the iron condor strategy performance metrics individually.

The OISUF performance metrics are extremely promising,

suggesting that the OISUF can be used by traders with diverse risk/return preferences to customize their option income strategy entry and exit requirements.

Please see the Resources Chapter at the end of this article for information on OISUF monthly-subscriptions.

6 - PRACTICAL CONSIDERATIONS

When testing strategies and filters, it is advantageous to use the largest applicable dataset to ensure representative results. That is why I used all 15,434 managed iron condor trades to calculate and evaluate the performance metrics for each of the trade filters presented in this article. The 15,000+ trades were generated daily from May 2004 to May 2016 using monthly SPX, RUT, and NDX options with 25 to 75 calendar days remaining until expiration. All trades were managed using the same objective set of trade rules and all trades included transaction costs of $1.00 per contract, per leg, per trade (entry and exit). I exported and scaled the results for each trade to a constant dollar amount at risk, applied an additional error-checking algorithm, and then calculated the aggregate performance metrics on the scaled and validated trade results.

In practice, we would obviously not enter a new iron condor trade every day on the SPX, RUT, and NDX due to the limited diversification benefits and because of the extraordinary amount of capital that would be required. This issue was not relevant during our initial filter testing, but becomes relevant now.

For further testing, I needed a realistic trade entry procedure that could be applied in practice, one that was fully consistent with the process used to generate the unfiltered dataset. To solve this problem, I used QuantyCarlo's one trade per expiration (1TPX) approach, instead of the one trade per signal (1TPS) methodology that has been used throughout this article.

The one trade per expiration (1TPX) framework only allowed a single trade (per underlying security) in a given days-to-expiration (DTE) window. The original window of 25 to 75 DTE was too wide to identify a specific position using the 1TPX methodology. As a result, I reduced the size of the window to 50 to 75 DTE for the 1TPX back-tests.

Once an iron condor position was established with 50 to 75 DTE, a new position could not be entered until the initial position was closed or fell below 50 DTE. This 1TPX testing procedure was used to calculate filtered and unfiltered performance metrics. No other changes were made to the original 1TPS testing methodology: same back-test period, same underlying securities, same transaction costs, same position model, same exit rules, and same scaling procedure.

Obviously, multiple iron condor positions could still be held simultaneously due to the use of the SPX, RUT, and NDX, but the number of positions was limited. QuantyCarlo preforms back-tests on each underlying security individually, not on a portfolio of securities. If I had wanted to limit the back-tests to a single open iron condor position, I would have had to manually reconstruct the trade entries on a daily basis, which would have been cumbersome at best and potentially erroneous at worst.

On the plus side, generating multiple simultaneous positions increased the number of trades, which made the 1TPX test results more representative. Using the 1TPX framework on filtered trades has another interesting implication; iron condor positions entered in one underlying security will not necessarily result in iron condor positions in the other underlying securities. The filters are applied individually, which results in optimal trade entries for each underlying security.

The importance of independent entries might not immediately seem obvious, mainly because the prices of the SPX, NDX, and RUT are very highly correlated. From 2000 to 2016, the price correlation pairs ranged from +0.941 to +0.977 (Figure 6.1). The average price correlation for pairs of the three indices was +0.955.

Figure 6.1: Price Correlation (RUT, SPX, NDX)			
Avg. = .955	RUT	SPX	NDX
RUT	1		
SPX	0.977	1	
NDX	0.948	0.941	1

While correlations of the index price pairs do approach +1.0, correlations of the filter values are typically lower. For example, the average correlation of the OIS Universal Filter scores was +0.865 (Figure 6.2), still high, but well below the average price correlation. The index-specific OISUF scores allowed iron condor positions to be entered on the optimal underlying security at the optimal time.

Figure 6.2: OIS Score Corr. (RUT, SPX, NDX)			
Avg. = .865	RUT OIS	SPX OIS	NDX OIS
RUT OIS	1		
SPX OIS	0.875	1	
NDX OIS	0.805	0.917	1

The first objective of this 1TPX back-test exercise was to calculate and evaluate the performance metrics for a replicable iron condor strategy. Since the resulting performance metrics would be calculated on a much smaller and somewhat arbitrary dataset, the goal was to ensure the results were *generally consistent* with those of the comprehensive dataset. The second objective was to provide a representative example of an iron condor strategy that could be replicated in practice. With those objectives in mind, let's review the 1TPX results for the equity indices.

1TPX Equity Index Results

The first column on the left-side of Figure 6.3 designates the OISUF entry conditions. Since we are now focusing on actual entry requirements, I limited the results in Figure 6.3 to OIS values that were greater than or equal to zero. The last three columns show the performance metrics (profit factor, percentage of winning trades, and average return on margin) for each filter condition.

To facilitate comparison with the filtered results, the first row in Figure 6.3 reports the performance metrics for the unfiltered trades. You will note that these results are different from the results for all 15,434 that were reported throughout this article.

The unfiltered results in Figure 6.3 use the 1TPX framework and only allow one trade per expiration window (per symbol). The 1TPX unfiltered profit factor was 2.03 (2.03 dollars of gains per dollar of losses). In addition, 84.89% of the unfiltered trades were profitable and the average return on margin was 3.27%. The 1TPX results were very similar to the unfiltered 1TPS results: profit factor of 2.10, 85.10% winning trades, and average return on margin of 3.22%.

As was the case with the 1TPS unfiltered trades, the performance metrics for the OISUF were an increasing function of the minimum OIS threshold score. Every increase in OIS score resulted in an increase in all three performance metrics – except for an OIS score of 80. It is interesting that we observed the same anomaly in the 1TPS results. The 1TPX correlations between the OIS score and the percentage of winning trades and return on margin were both very high: +0.971 and +0.936.

The performance metrics for the 1TPX data subset were impressive and were generally consistent with metrics from the comprehensive 1TPS dataset.

Figure 6.3: 1TPX - OIS Entry (RUT, SPX, NDX)			
Minimum OIS Score	Profit Factor	% Winning Trades	Avg. Return on Margin
N/A (ALL)	2.03	84.89%	3.27%
>= 0	2.64	87.53%	4.14%
>= 20	3.49	89.93%	4.93%
>= 40	4.19	91.33%	5.47%
>= 60	6.64	95.79%	6.44%
>= 80	5.00	95.12%	6.23%
>= 100	Infinite	100.00%	8.77%
OIS Score Correlation		0.971	0.936

1TPX EFA ETF Results

As I explained earlier, option income strategies on equity index options have a number of unique advantages: chronic overvaluation, liquidity, reduced transaction costs, tax advantages, etc. That is why I have focused exclusively on SPX, RUT, and NDX options in this article.

However, I wanted to include one non-index OIS Universal Filter example for illustration purposes. I used the identical QuantyCarlo iron condor trade plan with the 1TPX framework to generate the trade results for the iShares MSCI EAFE (EFA) exchange traded fund (ETF).

As you will recall, the OISUF requires historical and current price and volatility data, which means that it is only applicable to options on underlying securities that have their own volatility indices. Fortunately, the CBOE has greatly expanded the number of symbols with corresponding volatility indices. In addition, the CBOE currently provides free historical data downloads for all of their volatility indices.

I do not trade option income strategies on the EFA ETF; I selected the EFA at random from the list of qualifying ETFs. I knew it was liquid and had its own volatility index, but those were my only selection requirements. Based on your own experience, how would you expect the EFA iron condor results to differ from the equity index results?

* * *

I assumed the EFA iron condor performance metrics would probably suffer, primarily because of the greater drag of commission costs on a lower-priced ETF. In addition, there would be less demand for EFA options as a hedging vehicle, at least compared to options on the SPX, RUT, and NDX. As a result, EFA options might not be as persistently overvalued as options on the SPX, RUT, and NDX. Ideally, higher OIS scores would still translate to improved performance metrics.

With that premise in mind, let's proceed to the results. The format of the 1TPX EFA results in Figure 6.4 is the same as the format used in Figure 6.3. The first column on the left-side of Figure 6.4 shows the OISUF entry conditions, and the last three columns show the performance metrics.

The first row in Figure 6.4 reports the performance metrics for the unfiltered EFA trades. The unfiltered results in Figure 6.4 use the 1TPX framework and only allow one trade per expiration window. The 1TPX unfiltered profit factor was 0.86 (0.86 dollars of gains per dollar of losses). In addition, only 78.57% of the unfiltered trades were profitable and the average return on margin was -0.62%. The

1TPX unfiltered EFA iron condor strategy was *unprofitable*. The profit factor was less than 1.0 and the average return on margin was negative. The percentage of winning trades (78.57%) was much worse than the corresponding unfiltered equity index percentage (84.89%). These results are consistent with my expectations and demonstrate the importance of transaction costs on multi-leg option income strategies.

However, the more important question is whether the OISUF was effective in discriminating between favorable and unfavorable trade environments. As was the case with the SPX, RUT, and NDX trades, the performance metrics for the OISUF EFA trades were an increasing function of the minimum OIS threshold score. Every increase in OIS score resulted in an increase in all three performance metrics – except for the average return on margin at an OIS score of 40. In addition, the 1TPX correlations between the OIS score and the percentage of winning trades and return on margin were both very high: +0.975 and +0.914.

Perhaps the most compelling evidence of the effectiveness of the OISUF is that an OIS score of 100 produced 100% winning EFA iron condor trades. In other words, the OISUF was able to turn an unprofitable iron condor strategy into 100% winners.

Figure 6.4: 1TPX - OIS Entry (EFA)

Minimum OIS Score	Profit Factor	% Winning Trades	Avg. Return on Margin
N/A (ALL)	0.86	78.57%	-0.62%
>= 0	0.97	78.95%	-0.12%
>= 20	1.23	82.26%	0.76%
>= 40	1.10	83.33%	0.36%
>= 60	1.75	89.29%	1.95%
>= 80	2.41	92.31%	3.45%
>= 100	Infinite	100.00%	6.73%
OIS Score Correlation		0.975	0.914

There is no question that the performance metrics for the EFA iron condor trades are worse than the results for the SPX, RUT, and NDX trades. However, the OISUF was still able to identify the best possible environments for EFA iron condors and was able to overcome the punitive transaction costs to deliver attractive and profitable results at higher OIS levels.

Risk Management & Position Sizing

One of the key elements of risk management is position sizing. To calculate position size, we must first determine the appropriate amount of capital to risk on each trade. While there are a number of complex algorithms we could use, I would like to keep this as simple as possible. Most professional traders risk no more than one to two percent of their total capital on an individual trade.

Note, total capital at risk of one to two percent does not mean that the market value of each position only represents one to two percent of our total capital. It means that if the trade incurs the maximum loss (a function of our stop level and an estimate of extreme slippage), then we would lose no more than one to two percent of our total capital. What is slippage? Briefly, slippage represents the cost of selling the position at a price worse than where we plan to sell the position.

Limiting your losses to only one to two percent of total capital on each trade might seem overly conservative, but every trader eventually experiences a series of consecutive losses and it is very difficult to recover from losing a large percentage of your total capital, both emotionally and mathematically. To be successful, we must maintain sufficient capital to recover from our losses.

If we have a number of open iron condor positions and they are all highly correlated (e.g. on the SPX, RUT, and NDX), then we should also limit our aggregate risk on the entire group of correlated positions. If you would like a rule of thumb, risk no more than three to four percent of your total capital on the highly-correlated positions.

Here is a brief example of the position size calculation. If the maximum loss we could incur on a given trade equals 20% of the capital committed to the trade (*including extreme slippage*), and we are willing to lose no more than 1% of our total capital on the trade, the position size would equal 5% of our total capital (5% of total capital * 20% loss = loss of 1% of total capital).

A Brief Analogy

The results presented in this article have demonstrated that using discriminating filters to trade managed iron condors on the SPX, RUT, and NDX has historically delivered superior returns. The key to exploiting this advantage over time is to play the game repeatedly *when the odds are in our favor*. It is analogous to owning a casino in Las Vegas.

Casinos limit the size of each bet to ensure the probabilities work in their favor over time. They want blackjack players betting $25 on each hand and playing for hours and hours at a time. The casino's odds of winning increase dramatically as they play the game repeatedly. They do not want a player to walk in and place a $500,000 wager on a single hand of blackjack, just as we do not want to risk 50% of our total capital on a single transaction.

When we use discriminating filters to trade option income strategies on the equity indices, we are the casino; we have the statistical advantage. Two lessons from Vegas: place bets (trades) only when the odds are proven to be in your favor and limit your losses on every bet.

Hedging Exits

The position sizing example above raises an interesting problem. To complete the position size calculation, we must estimate the maximum loss that we *could* incur on each trade. Determining the exit rule is easy. We could plan to exit the trade when the loss equals 20% of required capital, but that maximum loss amount must include slippage. Any unexpected slippage would result in a realized loss greater than our maximum specified risk threshold. As a result, it is obviously critical to reduce slippage, but how do we do that, particularly when the options market is closed? If the market is closed, we cannot exit our option income positions.

To make matters worse, if the price of the underlying security was already approaching the strike price of the short put option in an iron condor, and the price of the underlying security gapped down overnight, the value of the iron condor could plummet, resulting in a massive amount of slippage (relative to the specified stop level) when the options market opened the next morning. Remember, iron condors become increasingly risky at the extremes, where they are very vulnerable to large discrete changes in price and implied volatility.

But are those price and IV changes really discrete? Overnight gaps appear discrete when looking exclusively at the closing and opening prices. However, there are markets that are open almost 24/7 that we could use to hedge our option income strategies when exit rules are triggered outside of regular trading hours: the financial futures markets.

Hedging can be confusing, so I created an example and used OptionVue to model the iron condor position. Let's assume we had an open SPX iron condor position. At the end of the trading day, the price of SPX was only a few ticks above the $1,940 strike price of the short put option. As you will recall from our trade plan, our exit rules require us to exit the iron condor when the price of the underlying security (SPX) touches either of the short strike prices.

If we followed the trade plan precisely, we would not exit the position before the close because the price of SPX had not touched the strike price of the short put option. However, keeping the position open would expose us to significant market risk and slippage. If the market gapped down overnight, we would not be able to exit the iron condor position until the options market opened the following morning. And the iron condor execution prices would be much worse than they would have been if we had exited when the SPX price had been $1,940.

I used OptionVue to model the hypothetical iron condor position at an SPX price of $1,940, the stop trigger price. The resulting position-Delta was positive 100 (Figure 6.5). A comprehensive analysis of the Greeks is beyond the scope of this article, but some explanation is required. Delta was originally zero when the trade was entered, but iron condors have negative Gamma. This means that when prices decline, Delta increases or becomes more bullish. Obviously this behavior is not desirable, but that is why iron condor traders are compensated with positive Theta. The decline in the price of SPX from its initial value to the strike price of the short put option ($1,940) caused the iron condor position-Delta to increase from zero to positive 100.

I used OptionVue to model the change in the value of the iron condor position in two extreme scenarios: 5% and 10% overnight declines in the price of SPX. The unhedged iron condor would have declined in value by $11,500 and $23,480 overnight. The iron condor would have already had an unrealized loss, so the cumulative losses would have been much greater. To put this in context, the original required capital was roughly $40,000.

Instead of accepting the overnight price risk as the SPX price approached the short strike price, we could have entered a conditional order to sell two E-mini S&P 500 futures contracts (symbol ES) if the price of the ES contract traded at or below $1,940. For simplicity purposes, I will assume in this example that the ES contract and SPX trade at the same price. Each ES contract controls 50 times the value of the S&P 500 index, so two ES contracts controls 100 times the value of the S&P index. The resulting Delta of the two-contract short ES position equals negative 100. As a result, selling two ES contracts would exactly offset the positive 100 position-Delta of the iron condor at the SPX price of $1,940.

The ES contract is one of the most liquid instruments in the world, even during times of extreme volatility. As a result, ES slippage is extremely small. The hypothetical sell order would have been filled almost instantaneously upon the price of the ES contract trading at $1,940. In the down 5% scenario, the gains in the E-mini short position would have offset $9,700 of the incremental $11,500 iron condor overnight loss. The hedged loss would have been $1,800 instead of $11,500 (Figure 6.5).

Similarly, in the down 10% scenario, the gains in the E-mini short position would have offset $19,400 of the incremental $23,480 iron condor overnight loss. The hedged loss would have been $4,080 instead of $23,480. The 0.25 round-trip bid-ask spread on two ES contracts would have only cost an additional $25. Not a bad investment, $25 to save $9,675 or $19,375 (Figure 6.5).

Figure 6.5: E-mini S&P 500 (ES) Futures Hedge			
Position	Position Delta @ SPX $1,940	Overnight Gain: SPX $1,843 (-5%)	Overnight Gain: SPX $1,743 (-10%)
Iron Condor @ Short Put Strike	100.0	-11,500	-23,480
Sell 2 E-mini S&P 500 Futures (ES)	-100.0	9,700	19,400
Hedged Position	0.0	-1,800	-4,080
Hedge Transaction Cost	N/A	-25	-25
Hedge Savings	N/A	9,675	19,375

Similar hedges can be executed using futures on the RUT and NDX indices. Futures hedges can even be executed when the market is open. Since we already know the stop trigger levels and can use tools like OptionVue to estimate index price levels at the specified loss targets, we can enter all conditional futures hedging orders in advance.

Even if we were sitting in front of our trading platform when an exit rule was triggered, the immediate futures Delta-hedge would give us time to work the limit order and exit the iron condor position at a reasonable price level. It takes time to get exit orders filled on iron condors when markets are volatile; futures hedges remove time pressure by instantaneously reducing market risk. Using futures to hedge option income strategy exits substantially reduces both transaction costs and market risk. Failing to use futures to hedge market risk when exit rules are triggered is one of the most frequent and significant oversights made by option income strategy traders. Mastering this technique could save you tens of thousands of dollars and greatly reduce your risk.

I should note that the back-test results in this article followed the iron condor trade plan exactly and did not use futures to hedge or reduce overnight market risk. As a result, many of the losing trades incurred very large slippage costs. While I did not back-test the iron condor strategy with the future hedge, I have no doubt that the results would have improved; risk would also have been reduced.

OISUF Exits & Adjustments

When I began researching the OIS Universal Filter, I originally intended to use the resulting OIS scores exclusively for entering OIS trades. I had not even planned to evaluate the results for OIS scores below zero. While writing this article, I had an epiphany: the OISUF algorithm could also be used to quantify when to exit and when to (or not to) adjust trades as well.

As shown in Figure 5.1, when OIS values are below negative 120, SPX, NDX, and RUT iron condor trades lose money, despite their inherent long-term advantage. As a result, creating a new rule to exit positions when OIS scores fall below negative 120, for example, can further improve strategy returns and reduce risk. I used the "EXR MinFilterExit" rule in the iron condor trade plan (Figure 2.4) to confirm that OIS scores could be used successfully for this purpose (not shown).

While adjustments are often detrimental to option income strategy returns, if you do plan to adjust your strategies, at least limit your adjustments to periods when the environment is favorable – when OIS scores are high. Do not risk even greater losses by adjusting losing strategies when the odds are against you.

Expanding the use of the OISUF algorithm to time entries, exits, and adjustments creates an objective OIS trade management system that is applicable throughout the life of every trade. I personally use the OISUF in conjunction with other filters to reduce the risks and enhance the returns of all of my option income strategies. The OISUF algorithm is proprietary, but monthly subscriptions are available through TraderEdge.Net. For more information on OISUF subscriptions and other trading tools, please see the Resources Chapter at the end of this article.

Conclusion

My goal in writing this article was to provide one of the most comprehensive evaluations of managed iron condor trades ever published. Even more important, I hoped to demonstrate detailed examples of how to create and test market-edge hypotheses using the recent advances in back-testing software.

The filtered performance metrics showed that it is possible to design and implement market-edge hypotheses and their corresponding discriminating filters to enhance option income strategy returns. Furthermore, the results revealed the remarkable advantages of combining multiple filters.

I hope you found the back-test results, analysis, practical examples, and insights to be both useful and educational. I encourage you to use these same tools and techniques to conduct your own research to elevate the performance of your option income strategies.

$* * *$

Please see the Resources Chapter for a description of reader discounts available on the products and services I personally use in my proprietary trading and research.

ABOUT THE AUTHOR

Brian Johnson designed, programmed, and implemented the first return sensitivity based parametric framework actively used to control risk in fixed income portfolios. He further extended the capabilities of this approach by designing and programming an integrated series of option valuation, prepayment, and optimization models.

Based on this technology, Mr. Johnson founded Lincoln Capital Management's fixed income index business, where he ultimately managed over $13 billion in assets for some of the largest and most sophisticated institutional clients in the U.S. and around the globe.

He later served as the President of a financial consulting and software development firm, designing artificial intelligence-based forecasting and risk management systems for institutional investment managers.

Mr. Johnson is now a full-time proprietary trader in options, futures, stocks, and ETFs primarily using algorithmic trading strategies. In addition to his professional investment experience, he also designed and taught courses in financial derivatives for both MBA and undergraduate business programs.

He is the author of two groundbreaking books on options: 1) *Option Strategy Risk / Return Ratios: A Revolutionary New Approach to Optimizing, Adjusting, and Trading Any Option Income Strategy*, and 2) *Exploiting Earnings Volatility: An Innovative New Approach to Evaluating, Optimizing, and Trading Option Strategies to Profit from Earnings Announcements*.

He has also written articles for the *Financial Analysts Journal*, *Active Trader*, and *Seeking Alpha* and he regularly shares his trading insights and research ideas as the editor of https://www.traderedge.net/.

Mr. Johnson holds a B.S. degree in finance with high honors from the University of Illinois at Urbana-Champaign and an MBA degree with a specialization in Finance from the University of Chicago Booth School of Business.

Email: BJohnson@TraderEdge.Net

RESOURCES

I write a wide range of free, informative articles on https://www.traderedge.net/. The goal of Trader Edge is to provide information and ideas that will help you enhance your investment process and improve your trading results. The articles cover many different topics: economic indicators, technical analysis, market commentary, options, futures, stocks, exchange traded funds (ETFs), strategy development, trade analysis, and risk management. You will find educational articles that appeal to the beginner, as well as advanced tools and strategies to support more experienced traders.

OIS Universal Filter Subscription

Trader Edge offers a monthly subscription to the proprietary Option Income Strategy Universal Filter (OISUF) algorithm, which was discussed in detail in this article. The OISUF algorithm is run via macros on an Excel spreadsheet, which requires a one-time download.

The spreadsheet is simple to use and has built-in macros to import free (as of this writing) Yahoo (price) and CBOE (IV) data. Data from alternative sources can also be copied and pasted as desired. The OISUF may be applied to options on any underlying security that has a corresponding volatility index. To learn more about OISUF subscriptions, please use the following link: https://traderedge.net/order/ois-universal-filter/

It is possible that the OISUF algorithm will be made available via subscription on various analytical or broker platforms in the future. If and when these tools become available, a notice will be posted on https://www.traderedge.net/.

OptionVue

Through our referral agreement, OptionVue is offering an exclusive 15% discount on the initial purchase of any annual subscription of any OptionVue product (including QuantyCarlo if it becomes available) and on all DiscoverOptions educational products. However, the discount is not available to current OptionVue clients with an active OptionVue subscription. Please use the coupon code "traderedge" (*lower case with no spaces or quotation marks*) to receive your 15% discount when ordering applicable products from OptionVue online or over the phone.

Visit http://www.optionvue.com/traderedge.html and take advantage of the exclusive 15% Trader Edge referral discount. If you would prefer to evaluate the OptionVue software before placing an order, the above link will also allow you to enroll in a free 14-day trial of OptionVue's option analytical platform.

QuantyCarlo is the most powerful, flexible, and intuitive dedicated option strategy back-testing software platform I have ever seen. QuantyCarlo subscriptions may soon be available through OptionVue.

Trading options without a comprehensive option analytical platform is not advisable and the OptionVue software is one of the most powerful tools available. Unlike most broker platforms, OptionVue evaluates both the horizontal and vertical volatility skews, resulting in much more realistic calculations and more accurate risk and valuation metrics. In addition, I worked with OptionVue to help them apply the aggregate implied volatility formula to quantify the effects of earnings volatility before and after earnings events in the OptionVue software.

The OptionVue software also includes a very powerful "Trade Finder" module, which is similar to the strategy optimization tool in the *Exploiting Earnings Volatility* Integrated spreadsheet. Trade Finder allows the user to specify an objective, strategy candidates, filters, and forecast adjustments and uses those inputs to search for the best possible strategy. Most important, *Trade Finder uses the aggregate implied volatility formula to accurately incorporate the effects of earnings volatility in its analysis.*

OptionVue also recently released a new subscription service specifically designed for "Earnings Plays." OptionVue's description of the five Earnings Play's strategies follows:

- Prime Movers: Stocks that make big moves - options tend to be undervalued.

- Prime Non-Movers: Stocks that make smaller-than-expected moves, options tend to be overvalued.

- Earnings Pairs: Two stocks in the same industry, only one of which is announcing earnings.

- Echoes - Two stocks in the same industry, with one announcing 1-18 days after the other.
- Runners - Stocks that tend to run in price after the earnings announcement.

This system is based on the hypothetical results actual trades would have experienced in the past and shows you a quality ranking for each trade along with its past success rate.

OptionVue offers real-time and historical option prices, which can be used to back-test option strategies, even with adjustments. OptionVue also offers subscriptions to proprietary strategies, including their VXX Trading System.

Finally, DiscoverOptions, the educational arm of OptionVue, offers one-on-one personal option mentoring from professional option traders with decades of experience.

OptionSlam.com

During the course of my research for my second book (*Exploiting Earnings Volatility*), I collaborated with the owners of OptionSlam.com on several enhancements for their site that will help all traders who use option strategies to trade earnings announcements.

Given the strong synergies between OptionSlam.com and the tools in my second book, OptionSlam.com has agreed to offer an exclusive 15% discount on annual INSIDER Memberships to my readers.

OptionSlam.com INSIDER Membership

The following benefits are provided to all INSIDER OptionSlam.com Members:
- View Earnings History of Individual Stocks
- View Volatility History of Individual Stocks
- View Straddle Tracking History of Individual Stocks
- View and Customize the Upcoming Earnings Filter
- View and Customize the Earnings Calendar
- View Weekly Implied Volatility Report
- View and Customize the Best Trending Stocks Report
- View and Customize the Current Straddles Report

- View and Customize the Historical Straddles Report
- View Trades from All Members
- Customize and Schedule Email Alerts of Personalized Reports
- Export Earnings Statistics to Excel

OptionSlam.com's historical earnings data provides all of the return and volatility data necessary to evaluate past earnings performance. The "Upcoming Earnings Filter" is a powerful and flexible tool that will help you efficiently identify both directional and non-directional trading candidates.

Visit https://www.optionslam.com/partner_info/traderedge and take advantage of the exclusive 15% Trader Edge referral discount.

CSI

Reliable prices are essential for developing and implementing systematic trading strategies. Commodity Systems Inc. (CSI) is one of the leading providers of market data and trading software for institutional and retail customers. Please use the following link to learn more about CSI's pricing subscriptions: https://csicheckout.com/cgi-bin/ua_order_form_nw.pl?referrer=TE.

I am a paying customer of QuantyCarlo, OptionVue, and CSI. My company, Trading Insights, LLC, has an affiliate referral relationship with OptionSlam.com, OptionVue, and CSI.

I hope you enjoy these tools and find them useful in your option trading and research.

www.ingramcontent.com/pod-product-compliance
Lightning Source LLC
Chambersburg PA
CBHW060621200326
41521CB00007B/837